U.S. Fish & Wildlife Service

Shared Commitments
To Conservation

2001 Accountability Report of the
U. S. Fish and Wildlife Service

I0434827

Table of Contents

I. The United States Fish and Wildlife Service

Page

History and Mission...iii
Organization of the Service iv
Message from the Acting Director vii

II. Supplementary Stewardship Information

Stewardship Lands 1
    Stewardship Lands and Facilities and Their Locations......................................1
    Uses of Stewardship Lands..2
    Revenue from Stewardship Assets...3
    Investments in Non-Federal Physical Property..3
    Net Change in Stewardship Land Acreage from 2000 to 2001 5
    Condition of Stewardship Lands 6
Heritage Assets 7
    Condition of Heritage Asset Facilities...7
    Cultural Resources..7
    Museum Collections..8
    Special Designations...8

III. Supplementary Information on Service Performance

The Year at a Glance 13
    Sustainability of Fish and Wildlife Populations...13
    Habitat Conservation...16
    Linking Wildlife and People...19
    Partnerships in Natural Resources 20
Facilities Management 20
    Equipment Replacement and Repair...22
Management Controls and Legal Compliance 22
Service Performance Trends..23
    Expected Changes in the Work of the Service..23
    Improving Delivery of Services..23

IV. Service Financial Performance

Message from the Chief Financial Officer..25
Financial Highlights 26
    Reporting the Aquatic Resources Trust Fund on this Year s
        Financial Statements...26
    Environmental Cleanup Liabilities...26
    Service Financial Performance 26
    Improving Financial Transaction Processes and Results 26
    Improving Cost Recovery and Cost Allocation Practices...................................27
Limitations of the Financial Statements..29
Principal Financial Statements 30
Notes to the Principal Financial Statements...35
Combining Statement of Budgetary Resources...49
Independent Auditors Report..50

The United States Fish and Wildlife Service

History and Mission

As an asset of tremendous environmental, recreational, and economic importance, this Nation's fish and wildlife resources represent a vital part of our natural heritage - one that is facing increasing pressures every day. For this reason, the mission of the U.S. Fish and Wildlife Service (Service) grows more complex and critical every day. As the Service continues to look for new and better ways to conserve, protect, and enhance fish and wildlife and their habitat, its major responsibilities remain focused on migratory birds, endangered species, certain marine mammals, and freshwater and anadromous fish.

History of the Service

The Service's origins date back to 1871 when Congress established the U.S. Fish Commission to study the decrease in the Nation's food fish and recommend ways to reverse the decline. Placed under the Department of Commerce in 1903, it was renamed the Bureau of Fisheries. Meanwhile Congress created an Office of Economic Ornithology in the Department of Agriculture in 1885 to study the food habits and migratory patterns of birds, especially those that had an effect on agriculture. After several more name changes, this office was renamed the Bureau of Biological Survey in 1905.

The Bureaus of Fisheries and Biological Survey were transferred to the Department of the Interior in 1939, and in 1940, were combined and named the Fish and Wildlife Service. Further reorganization came in 1956 when the Fish and Wildlife Act created the United States Fish and Wildlife Service and established within the agency two separate bureaus - Commercial Fisheries and Sport Fisheries and Wildlife.

The Bureau of Commercial Fisheries was transferred to the Department of Commerce in 1970 and is now known as the National Marine Fisheries Service. The Bureau of Sport Fisheries and Wildlife remained in Interior. In 1974, the "Bureau" name was dropped and the agency is now simply called the U.S. Fish and Wildlife Service. In 1993, the

Service's research activities were transferred to the U.S. Geological Survey.

Today, the Service employs approximately 7,900 personnel and is supported by a volunteer force of approximately 36,000 citizens. Although the Service is headquartered in Washington, D.C., over 80 percent of the workforce is located in local communities across the Nation at over 700 field stations and supported by seven regional offices. As a result of our community level of involvement, the majority of Service employees has routine contact with the public.

Mission of the Service

The Service's mission is working with others to conserve, protect and enhance fish, wildlife, and plants and their habitats for the continuing benefit of the American people.

Since before recorded history, fish and wildlife resources in North America have been an integral part of human life. We know that the earliest Americans depended on fish and wildlife for both life sustenance and spiritual nourishment. The kinship of aboriginal Americans to these resources is seen today in their religious and cultural activities. The sea turtle is viewed as the symbol of eternal

life with the great creator. Salmon and other anadromous fishes were and still are celebrated as symbols of the renewal of life. Wildlife served as the spiritual connection with ones ancestors and the creator of all life.

When settlers came to America, they found a land teeming with wildlife. Like Native Americans, they depended on the land's rich wildlife heritage for food and clothing. Colonies were located near rivers for commerce and travel and for a rich supply of fish and wildlife for food. The new settlers fully intended that freedom to hunt for food and to secure water for life would be the right of all, regardless of heritage or status. The framers of our Constitution recognized this and placed great emphasis on natural rights and natural laws. Because of the American ideal to respect fish and wildlife as a resource available for the use and enjoyment of all, it is revered as a public trust resource - a resource deserving the public's attention and participatory guidance. The United States continues to refine the body of case law and statutes governing the stewardship of fish and wildlife resources.

Communities and people throughout the United States have a strong commitment to the fish and wildlife resources today. Many communities realize tremendous economic benefits from tourism and visitors that come specifically to enjoy watching and pursuing fish and wildlife. Hunting and fishing remain strong components of community culture all along the great river systems of the Nation. Americans value and respect their natural resource heritage.

The U.S. Fish and Wildlife Service has the privilege of being the primary agency responsible for the protection, conservation, and renewal of these resources for this and future generations. We accept this responsibility and challenge with optimism and resolve to pass along to future generations of stewards a fish and wildlife resource heritage that is as strong or stronger than when it was entrusted to us.

Organization of the Service

As shown in the accompanying organization chart, the Directorate of the Service is comprised of the Director and Deputy Director, eight Assistant Directors, the Chief of the National Wildlife Refuge System, all located in Washington, D.C., and seven Regional Directors, located throughout the United States. Service headquarters is located in Washington, D.C. and Arlington, Virginia, with field units in Denver, Colorado, and Shepherdstown, West Virginia. Regional Offices are located throughout the United States. Region 1, located in Portland, Oregon, serves California, Hawaii, Idaho, Nevada, Oregon, and Washington, as well as the Trust Territories of the Pacific. Region 2, located in Albuquerque, New Mexico, serves Arizona, New Mexico, Oklahoma and Texas. Region 3, located in Minneapolis, Minnesota, serves Indiana, Illinois, Iowa, Michigan, Minnesota, Missouri, Ohio, and Wisconsin. Region 4, located in Atlanta, Georgia, serves Alabama, Arkansas, Florida, Georgia, Kentucky, Louisiana, Mississippi, North Carolina, South Carolina, and Tennessee, as well as Puerto Rico and Virgin Islands. Region 5, located in Hadley, Massachusetts, serves Connecticut, Delaware, Maine, Massachusetts, Maryland, New Hampshire, New Jersey, New York, Pennsylvania, Rhode Island, Virginia, Vermont, and West Virginia, and the District of Columbia. Region 6, located in Denver, Colorado, serves Kansas, Montana, North Dakota, South Dakota, Nebraska, Colorado, Utah and Wyoming. Region 7, located in Anchorage, Alaska serves the entire state of Alaska.

In the Department of the Interior, the Service's Director reports to the Assistant Secretary for Fish and Wildlife and Parks and has direct line authority over Service headquarters and seven regional offices. Assistant Directors and the Chief of the National Wildlife Refuge System provide policy, program management and administrative support to the Director. Regional Directors guide policy and program implementation through their field structures and coordinate activities with Service partners.

United States Fish and Wildlife Service
Organization

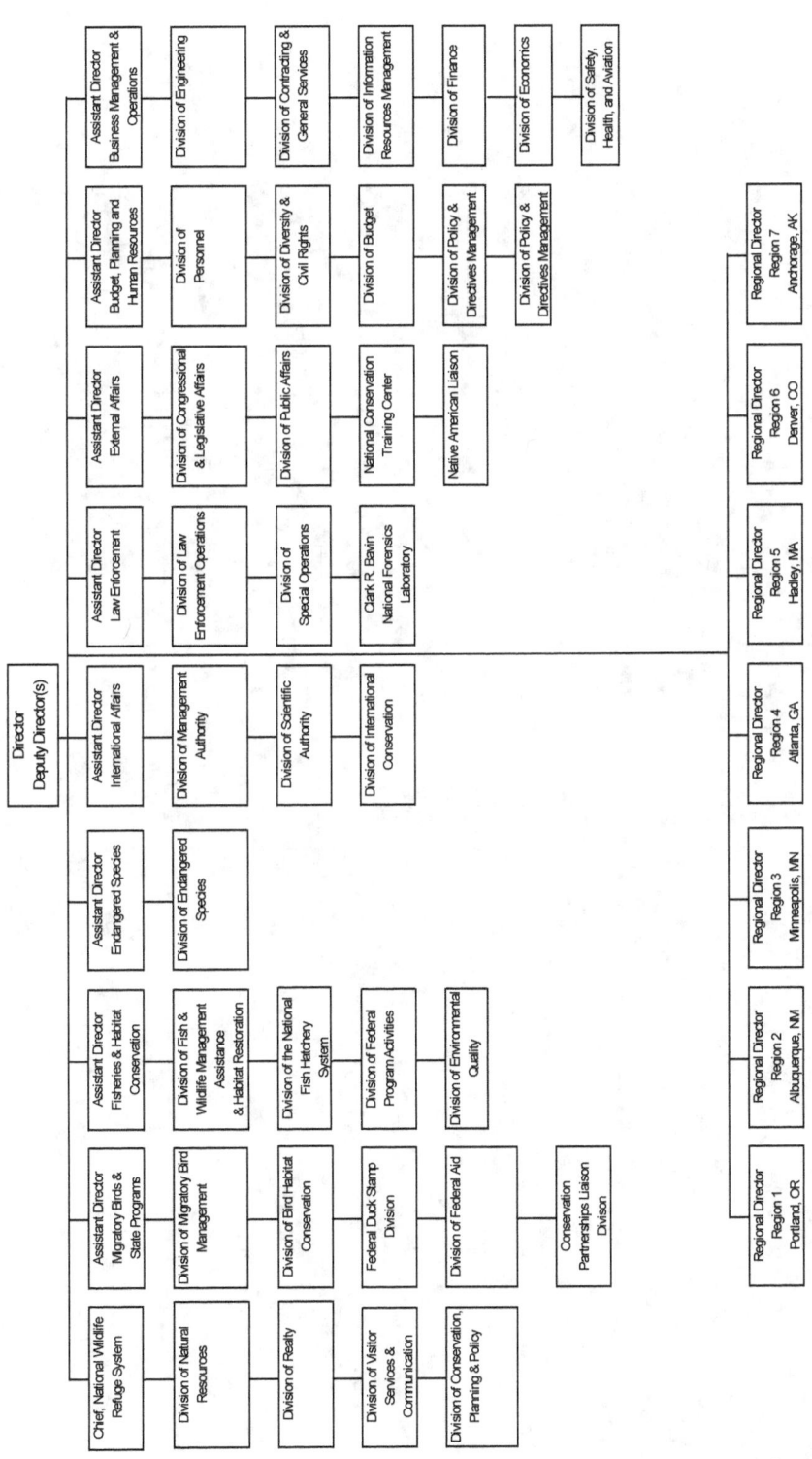

Message from the Acting Director

I am pleased to present the U.S. Fish and Wildlife Service's 2001 Accountability Report. This report highlights our accomplishments for Fiscal Year 2001, both in financial and non-financial terms, to give you a better understanding of what we do, how we do it, and how we manage resources to conserve fish, wildlife, and plants and their habitats for the benefit of this and future generations.

We are primarily a scientific organization, composed of fisheries and wildlife biologists, wildlife law enforcement officers, botanists, ecologists, and outdoor recreation interpretation specialists and planners. The challenge for these professionals is not simply controlling the numbers of waterfowl harvested or fish caught. Service employees work with our partners – private citizens, local communities, State and Federal agencies, Native American Tribes, foreign governments and others – to promote a coordinated domestic and international strategy to protect, restore and enhance the world's diverse wildlife.

This report shows how the Service faces complex biodiversity and biological sustainability issues and implements the directives of Congress and the American people in our shared commitment to conservation. It is through these efforts that present and future generations can experience nature as it is, rather than through museum exhibitions of nature as it was.

We hope you will find this report both enlightening and informative.

Marshall P. Jones, Jr.
Acting Director
U.S. Fish & Wildlife Service

Supplementary Stewardship Information

By law and treaty, the Service has national and international management and law enforcement responsibilities for migratory birds, threatened and endangered species, fisheries and many marine mammals. Also, the Service assists State and Tribal governments and other Federal agencies in protecting America's fish and wildlife resources. Further, the Service manages more than 95 million acres in the National Wildlife Refuge System (NWRS) and the National Fish Hatchery System (NFHS). These lands and the fish and wildlife resources they support are valued for their environmental and cultural resources, educational and scientific benefits, recreational and scenic values, and the revenue they provide to the Federal Government, States, and counties.

Stewardship Lands
Stewardship Lands and Facilities and Their Locations
The Service manages land in all 50 States, some of the Pacific Islands, the U.S. Virgin Islands, Guam, and Puerto Rico. More than 80 percent of the acreage of the Service's land holdings are in Alaska. Lands within the NWRS include more than 537 refuge units, 202 Waterfowl Production Area Counties, and 50 Coordination Areas. Lands and facilities within the NFHS comprise 70 National Fish Hatcheries, seven Fish Technology Centers, nine Fish Health Centers, and one Historical National Fish Hatchery, located in 34 States. This represents a change from FY 2000 by counting Dexter (NM), Mora (NM), San Marcos (TX), Bears Bluff (SC), and Lamar (PA) National Fish Hatcheries as separate units rather than as complexes with other facilities. Also, Berkshire NFH, Massachusetts, was not counted as it is no longer operated by the Service.

Figure 1 displays the acreage owned by the Service. Lands are acquired through a variety of methods, including withdrawal from the public domain, fee title purchase, transfer of jurisdiction, donation, or gift. Figure 2 shows the percentage of stewardship lands acquired through these different methods. Lands are purchased through two primary sources of funding, the Migratory Bird Conservation Fund and the Land and Water Conservation Fund.

Figure 1

Annual Stewardship Information for the Years Ended September 30, 2001 and 2000
(Acres in Thousands)

	2001		2000	
	Sites	Acres	Sites	Acres
National Wildlife Refuge System:				
National Wildlife Refuges	537	89,146	530	87,790
Coordination Areas	50	197	50	197
Waterfowl Production Areas	202	728	201	725
Total NWRS	789	90,071	781	88,712
Total NFHS	87	12	83	12
Total FWS Lands	**876**	**90,083**	**864**	**88,724**

Stewardship of the Nation's fishery and aquatic resources, through the NFHS, has been a core responsibility of the Service for over 120 years.

Large mouth bass fishing

Uses of Stewardship Lands
Lands managed within the NWRS are used to conserve and manage fish, wildlife and plant resources for the benefit of present and future generations. The protected habitat is as diverse as the wild things living there. Service stewardship lands protect tundra, grasslands, deserts, forests, rivers, marshes, swamps, and remote islands - virtually every type of habitat and landscape found in the United States.

to fish, or to study and learn about wildlife and their needs.

Stewardship of the Nation's fishery and aquatic resources, through the NFHS, has been a core responsibility of the Service for more than 120 years. Although the Service does not own all the lands and facilities in the NFHS, the Service participates in managing units within the NFHS, which comprises National Fish Hatcheries, Fish Health Centers, and Fish Technology Centers.

Figure 2

Methods and Percentage of Stewardship Lands Acquired

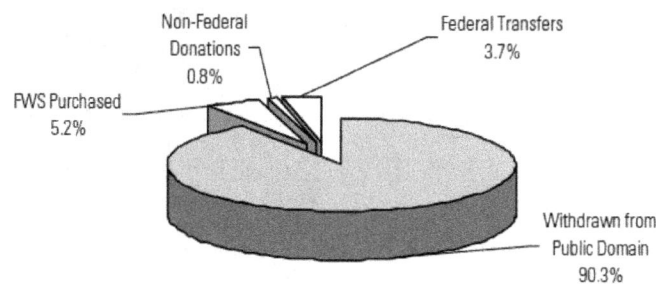

Non-Federal Donations 0.8%

FWS Purchased 5.2%

Federal Transfers 3.7%

Withdrawn from Public Domain 90.3%

The fish, wildlife and plants that live on refuges are the heritage of a wild America that was, and continues today in the NWRS. The refuge system watches over more than 700 species of birds, 220 species of mammals, 250 reptile and amphibian species, more than 200 species of fish, at least 260 threatened and endangered species, and countless species of invertebrates and plants. They come as flocks, herds, coveys, gaggles, schools, pairs and loners. The Service protects, restores, and manages our fish, wildlife, plant, land, and water heritage. We count it, study it, band it, mark it, and reintroduce it and we let wildlife reproduce naturally by managing its home and its habitat. On many refuges the Service must restore what was ditched, drained and cleared and actively manage wetlands, grasslands, forests, and to a lesser extent, croplands to provide the variety of habitat needed by diverse fish and wildlife species. Control of invasive and exotic pest plants and animals is essential to retain or restore native fish, wildlife, and plants. More than three million acres of NWRS lands are restored and enhanced each year. While the needs of fish and wildlife must come first, refuges welcome those who want to enjoy the natural world, to observe or photograph wildlife, to hunt or

Many of our hatcheries serve as outdoor laboratories for school groups, environmental organizations, and universities. Visitor centers on hatcheries provide public educational opportunities for approximately three million visitors each year. Fish Health Centers focus on cooperative work conducted by Federal, State and Tribal fishery managers to identify and control fish pathogens and diseases, particularly in wild stocks. Fish Technology Centers emphasize scientific management of fish stocks and aquatic communities by improving technologies in fish propagation, broodstock management, stock assessment, and aquaculture. NFHS lands also provide refugia, technology development and captive propagation for more than 30 species of threatened and endangered plants and animals, from Texas wild rice to Wyoming toads to Ozark cavefish. In addition to conservation, restoration, and management of fish and wildlife resources and their habitats, the NFHS provides recreational opportunities to the public, such as fishing, hiking, and bird watching.

All programs contributing to stewardship actions on Service lands are tied to supporting the Service's mission -

'working with others to conserve, protect and enhance fish, wildlife, and plants and their habitats for the continuing benefit of the American people.' The Service also recognizes the role that our Federal, State, Tribal, and private partners play in conserving stewardship resources.

Revenue from Stewardship Assets
The Recreation Fee Demonstration Program continues to be a highly successful endeavor for the participating units of the NWRS. Three new sites were added in FY 2001, including Big Branch Marsh NWR, Louisiana; Reelfoot NWR Complex, Tennessee; and Washita NWR, Oklahoma. The participating sites collected approximately $3.7 million, and at least 80 percent of that is returned to the refuges that collected it. Refuges use these funds to enhance visitor experiences and improve visitor services through restoring and maintaining trails, developing interpretive programs, improving signs, and creating accessible wildlife observation platforms.

Also, the Service makes payments to counties in which Service lands and holdings are located. Funding for these payments is derived from a combination of annual appropriations and revenues generated through the sale of products from Service lands incidental to habitat management, such as timber and oil and gas receipts. Payments to counties in FY 2001 totaled more than $15.6 million.

Investments in Non-Federal Physical Property
Stewardship investment in non-Federal physical property refers to expenses incurred by the Federal Government for the purchase, construction, or the major renovation of physical property owned by State or local governments. Such investments include major additions, alterations or replacements; the purchase of major equipment; and, the purchase or improvements of other physical assets. Expenses for maintenance and operations are not considered investments. In FY 2001, the Service estimates that it provided between $178 million and $192 million in grants to State and local governments that resulted in the purchase, construction or major renovation of physical property they own.

Service programs awarding grants to State and local governments resulting in the purchase, construction or major renovation of their physical property are: Federal Aid Grants - The Service's Federal Aid in Sport Fish Restoration

and the Federal Aid in Wildlife Restoration Programs are mainstays of State fish and wildlife resource management efforts. Excise taxes, collected from manufacturers of equipment used in hunting and fishing, shooting ranges, and on motorboat fuels, are deposited into a trust fund and Treasury account for investment. After appropriate deductions, they are apportioned to each State. In FY 2001, apportionments of Sport Fish and Wildlife Restoration funding for the States totaled more than $442 million. The last five-year average apportionment to the States was more than $176 million for wildlife and more than $247 million for sport fish restoration. In FY 2001, the States reported spending between $37.6 million and $45.3 million of Sport Fish Restoration and between $36.9 million and $41.66 million of Wildlife Restoration on non-Federal physical property.

The Boating Infrastructure Grant Program provided approximately $8 million in FY 2001 to States and territories to construct support facilities for boats more than 26 feet in length. This grant program will provide a total of $32 million between FY 2000 and FY 2003.

The Clean Vessel Act provides funding to States and territories for facilities used by recreational boaters to dispose of sewage in an environmentally sound manner. In FY 2001, the Service provided almost $10 million to States and territories under this program of which the States reported spending between $1.4 million and $2.1 million on non-Federal physical property.

The Wildlife Conservation and Appreciation Fund provides funding to States and territories for the management, conservation and protection for wildlife species not normally hunted or not considered to be endangered or threatened. In FY 2001, the Service provided between $1.1 million and $1.94 million to States and territories under this program.

Coastal Wetlands Conservation Grants - Through the National Coastal Wetlands Conservation Grant Program, the Service provides resources to States to protect and restore coastal habitats. In FY 2001, approximately $15 million in matching grants was provided to coastal States for acquisition, restoration and enhancement of coastal wetlands.

All programs contributing to stewardship actions on Service lands are tied to supporting the Service's mission - 'working with others to conserve, protect and enhance fish, wildlife, and plants and their habitats for the continuing benefit of the American people.'

USFWS Photo

Bison Bull

Cooperative Endangered Species Conservation Program - Under Section 6 of the Endangered Species Act, support from the Cooperative Endangered Species Fund is provided for species and habitat recovery on non-Federal lands. These grants provide funding for monitoring delisted species, assist in building conservation partnerships, and facilitate the transition of authority from the Service to States and territories. A description of these grants is provided in the next two paragraphs.

Hollingsworth/USFWS Photo

Speckled Dace, Ash Meadows NWR, NV

Recovery Land Acquisition Program - The Service awards funds to the States for projects through a competitive process for Recovery Land Acquisition. Land is purchased under this Program that is consistent with habitat prescribed in endangered species recovery plans and set aside in perpetuity. If the species is delisted due to recovery, then habitat acquired as part of the recovery process is maintained to ensure that habitat loss does not contribute to species decline in the future. Land set aside for the recovery of one species often provides benefits for other listed species or species of concern thereby providing numerous benefits to other than the "targeted" species. In FY 2001, the Service awarded approximately $10.4 million to in the States of Arkansas, California, Hawaii, Illinois, Indiana, Kentucky, Maine, Minnesota, Nebraska, Tennessee and Utah under this program.

Habitat Conservation Plan (HCP) Land Acquisition Program - An HCP agreement between a landowner and the Service allows a landowner to incidentally take a threatened or endangered species in the course of otherwise lawful activities when the landowner agrees to conservation measures that will mitigate and minimize the impact of the taking. The HCP Land Acquisition Grants allow for continued land development and use and at the same time provide conservation measures for threatened and endangered species. Some large HCP Land Acquisition Grants involve multiple species and an entire community. They are excellent examples of how conservation is a partnership between private citizens and local, State and Federal agencies. In FY 2001, the Service awarded approximately $67.8 million to the States of California, Florida, Georgia, Maryland, Montana, North Carolina, Texas, Utah, Washington, and Wisconsin under this program.

The Service also administers other grant programs that benefit conservation efforts not only in the United States, but throughout the world. Collectively, the grant programs administered by the Service are provided to State and foreign governments, conservation organizations and other partners. These grants are for the purposes of conserving and managing fish and wildlife resources, providing conservation education, providing on-the-ground support for species conservation, assisting partners in managing key fish and wildlife species affected by global trade practices, enforcing national and international conservation laws and treaties, and enhancing the work of the global conservation community in preserving valuable habitat and fish and wildlife resources throughout the nation and the world. More information on the comprehensive work of the Service can be found in the Supplementary Information section entitled, "The Year at a Glance."

Net Change in Stewardship Land Acreage from 2000 to 2001
The Service acquired fee title or other interests in approximately 1.2 million acres of stewardship lands. These lands provide permanent protection for valuable wetland, riparian, coastal and upland habitat for fish, wildlife and plant species, including threatened and endangered species.

The Service is committed to the preservation of biodiversity and the management of resources on an ecosystem basis. Land acquisition and balancing of the NWRS and NFHS resources are important tools used by the Service for attaining these goals.

The Service increased the number of units in the National Wildlife Refuge System in FY 2001 from 530 in FY 2000 to 537 in FY 2001. Seven new refuges were established – the Oahu Forest NWR in Hawaii, Kingman Reef NWR in the Pacific, Assabet River NWR in Massachusetts, Palmyra Atoll NWR in the Pacific, Vieques NWR in Puerto Rico, Dakota Tallgrass Prairie Wildlife Management Area (WMA) in North and South Dakota, and Caddo Lake NWR in Texas. In addition, another refuge was created when one of the two existing divisions in the Tallahatchie NWR in Tennessee was renamed the Coldwater NWR. One overlay refuge was terminated when the Service's agreement with the Corps of Engineers for secondary jurisdiction at the Pocasse NWR in South Dakota was terminated.

The Oahu Forest National Wildlife Refuge was established in the northern Koolau Mountains in the County of Honolulu, on the Island of Oahu, Hawaii. The refuge supports a diversity of native plants and animals including four species of endangered tree snails, 17 endangered plants, and rare birds such as the proposed endangered native Oʻahu ʻElepaio and the Hawaiian Owl.

The Kingman Reef National Wildlife Refuge was established in the Central

Common Puffin

James Leupold/USFWS

Pacific Ocean. The refuge supports a diversity of marine life including reef fishes, corals, sharks, seaweeds, giant clams, crabs, lobsters, manta rays, and other wildlife including migratory seabirds and threatened green sea turtles. Establishment of this refuge allows the Service to conserve this outstanding coral reef ecosystem and its associated marine habitats and wildlife.

Desert Tortoise, Glamis, CA

© J. Rorabough/USFWS

Waterfall, Chattachoochee River, GA

The Service is committed to the preservation of biodiversity and the management of resources on an ecosystem basis.

Fishing in North Carolina

Assabet River National Wildlife Refuge was established on a portion of an Army training facility in Massachusetts. These uplands are a mix of forest and grasslands, while the wetlands in the River's floodplain consist mostly of wooded swamp. Part of the Assabet River System was listed as a priority wetland by the Environmental Protection Agency, as a priority focus area under the North American Waterfowl Management Plan, and in the Regional Wetland Concept Plan under the Emergency Wetlands Resources Act.

The Palmyra Atoll National Wildlife Refuge was also established in the Central Pacific Ocean. This refuge supports migratory seabirds and shorebirds, and a rich diversity of marine species including giant clams, more than 100 species of corals, a variety of other marine invertebrates, algae, hundreds of species of fish, endangered and threatened sea turtles, and marine mammals. It includes the largest stand of intact native Pisonia rainforest in the United States.

The Vieques National Wildlife Refuge was established on the Island of Vieques, Puerto Rico by transfer from the Secretary of Navy. The refuge contains several ecologically distinct habitats including beaches, coastal lagoons, mangroves wetlands, and upland forested areas. The marine environment surrounding the refuge consists of coral reefs and sea grass beds. The refuge is home to at least four plants and 10 animals on the Federal endangered species list including the West Indian manatee, the brown pelican, and four species of sea turtles.

The Dakota Tallgrass Prairie WMA was established in 3 counties in eastern North Dakota and 23 counties in eastern South Dakota. It protects high-quality tallgrass prairie habitat for more than 300 species of plants, 113 species of butterflies, 35 species of reptiles and amphibians, 60 species of mammals, and 260 species of birds.

The Caddo Lake NWR was established as an "overlay" refuge in Harrison County, Texas, which protects the declining palustrine forested wetlands that are part of a Ramsar Wetland of International Significance with up to 224 species of birds, 22 species of amphibians, 46 species of reptiles, and 93 species of fish.

The Coldwater River National Wildlife Refuge was created from one of the two existing divisions of the Tallahatchie NWR that was established in 1991 in Grenada, Quitman and Tallahatchie Counties, Mississippi. The creation of the Coldwater River NWR from the existing Black Bayou division will allow the lands and programs of both units to be managed and administered more efficiently and eliminate confusion when we inform the public of our management activities on each refuge.

Condition of Stewardship Lands
The Service has stewardship responsibilities for the lands and associated heritage assets under its jurisdiction. These responsibilities are intertwined with the condition of the fish, wildlife and plant resources that depend on Service stewardship assets for their well-being and, in some cases, their survival. Service resources are managed or maintained in a state or condition so that fish and wildlife resources are conserved and protected for the continuing benefit of Americans and in a manner consistent with the requirements of conservation designations.

Stewardship lands managed by the Service include refuges, fish hatcheries, wilderness areas, National Natural Landmarks, Wild and Scenic Rivers, and other special designations. They are used and managed in accordance with the explicit purposes of the statutes authorizing their acquisition or designation and directing their use and management. Lands placed in the land conservation systems managed by the Service are protected as long as they remain in the NWRS and the NFHS. As new lands enter these conservation systems, they are managed to maintain their natural state, to mitigate adverse effects of actions previously conducted by others, or to enhance existing conditions to improve benefits to fish and wildlife resources. The Service safeguards the stewardship values of the lands it administers through management actions taken on individual refuges and hatcheries; however, such actions are taken in consideration of the needs and purposes of the entire NWRS and NFHS. The NWRS and the NFHS systems provide integrated habitat and life support for both permanent resident populations and for migratory populations needing temporary stopover sites to rest, breed, feed, and to survive nationwide and, in some cases, worldwide seasonal migrations. While some individual units of stewardship lands can be improved at any time during their management cycles, the condition of the stewardship assets as a whole, protected by inclusion in either the NWRS and the NFHS, is sufficient to support the mission of the Service and the statutory purposes for which these conservation systems were authorized.

The Service assesses the condition of its stewardship lands and resources by monitoring habitat characteristics and determining whether management actions are needed to change those characteristics to benefit their usefulness to fish and wildlife resources. The Service monitors habitat condition through assessment studies to determine habitat quality. Based on such studies, the Service may determine that specific management and protection actions are necessary. Sites may be restored to improve habitat for specific species or moist soils and wetlands may be managed to improve habitat productivity. New or different integrated pest management practices may be used to benefit stressed refuge resources or law enforcement actions may be increased to prevent potential or discovered illegal use of refuge resources. A wide variety of techniques, such as grazing, haying, prescribed burning, and farming, necessary to meet local and System resource management goals, may be used by the Service. Thus, condition of stewardship lands managed by the Service is not in a static state. Land or habitat conditions may change, either through the imposition of management techniques or through natural stressors or processes acting on those lands. The Service's goal is to provide habitat that optimizes the usefulness of stewardship lands to benefit fish and wildlife resources.

Heritage Assets

Some of the Service's stewardship lands fall into the category of heritage assets. Heritage assets are those lands, buildings and structures, and associated resources recognized for their ecological, cultural, historical and scientific importance. Heritage assets also include cultural resources, such as archaeological resources and historic properties, and museum collections derived from lands and facilities managed by the Service.

Heritage assets include those lands managed by the Service that carry overlay or special designations authorized by Congress, the President, the Secretary of the Interior or by conventions of national or international stature. Thus, heritage assets also include Wilderness Areas, Wild and Scenic Rivers, National Natural Landmarks, and Wetlands of International Importance. Such lands managed by the Service protect valuable natural and cultural resources in every State and a number of U.S. territories and possessions. The protection of these lands benefits not only the Nation's fish and wildlife populations, but helps preserve important elements of our past and cultural diversity. The condition of all lands managed by the Service, including those lands represented by special designations of national or international importance, is discussed in previous paragraphs as well as in this section. Special designations are managed or maintained in a manner that preserves the values that originally qualified these assets for their special designations. The status and condition of cultural resources, museum collections, and facilities defined as heritage assets are discussed below.

Condition of Heritage Asset Facilities
Heritage assets are defined as property, plant and equipment of historical, natural, cultural, educational, or artistic significance. The Service defines those sites and facilities under its administration that have nationally recognized historical or cultural designations as heritage assets. Please refer to the Facilities Management section of the Supplementary Information on Service Performance in this report for details on the deferred maintenance needs of all facilities managed by the Service. The overall condition of facilities managed by the Service, which includes heritage assets, is documented to be in poor condition and in need of repair.

Cultural Resources
Lands managed by the Service are particularly important for protecting significant sites associated with the Nation's prehistory and history. By closely examining their geographic distribution, an obvious pattern unfolds. Service lands are located along major river corridors, coastal areas, or in association with wetlands and North America's migratory bird flyways. Humans have used these same areas for thousands of years for transportation,

Snow Geese, Bombay Hook NWR, DE

Stefan Dobert/USFWS

The Service's goal is to provide habitat that optimizes the usefulness of stewardship lands to benefit fish and wildlife resources.

Kodiak NWR, Alaska

Bruce Batten/USFWS

Banding Peregrine Chicks

Shawn Padgett/USFWS

Wilderness is where the earth and its community of life are untrammeled by human beings...

American Widgeon

A.A. Allen/USFWS

settlement, and subsistence. Archaeological and historic sites located on these lands contribute important information on changes to habitat and wildlife over time and offer fish and wildlife conservation partnership opportunities with local communities and tribes.

As of FY 2001, the Service documented more than 11,000 archaeological and historic sites on a small percentage of its lands and estimates that it is responsible for tens of thousands of additional sites yet to be identified. Cultural properties range in age and type from the Sod House historic ranch on the Malheur NWR, Oregon to early 20th Century military fortifications in Fort Dade on Egmont Key NWR, Florida to a 10,000 year old archaeological site on a refuge in Tennessee, to a segment of the Lewis and Clark National Historic Trail on the Charles M. Russell NWR, Montana, to the Victorian-era historic buildings on the D.C. Booth Historic Fish Hatchery in South Dakota. Cultural properties managed by the Service reflect our Nation's rich heritage and diversity.

Of the total number of known cultural resources, an estimated 84 sites or districts have been listed in the National Register of Historic Places. The Service also manages nine National Historic Landmarks designated by the Secretary of the Interior to protect and recognize sites of exceptional importance.

Service-wide information on the number and status of archaeological properties is summarized each year for the Secretary of the Interior's report to Congress required by the Archaeological Resources Protection Act. The physical condition of cultural resources managed by the Service varies tremendously, depending on location, maintenance, use, and type of resource. While no comprehensive assessment is available, the Service is developing guidance and criteria to begin collecting information. The Service estimates that a minimum of 10 years is required to assess the condition of identified cultural resources under its jurisdiction.

Museum Collections

Service museum collections consist of approximately 4.4 million objects maintained in 150 offices or on loan to 226 non-Federal repositories for study and long-term care. The overall condition of Service museum collections is adequate to good. Collections consist of

archaeological materials excavated from Service managed cultural resources; paleontological collections; objects and documents associated with the agency's history; wildlife art; and, wildlife, fisheries, and botanical specimens. Service collections are used for educational and interpretive programs, research on changes to habitat and wildlife, and maintaining the history and traditions of the Service's programs and employees.

The Service continues to accession new museum collections each year, primarily as a result of the scientifically controlled excavation of archaeological sites on its lands. More than 82 percent of the Service's collections are maintained on loan by museums and other institutions. The Service ensures that these collections are safeguarded through compliance with the Secretary of the Interior's curation standards found in 36 CFR 79. Institutions must maintain the appropriate environmental, record-keeping, and security controls in order to qualify for maintaining Federal collections. Loan agreements signed by the Service and institutions create the basis for ensuring the perpetual care of these valuable materials.

Information standards for tracking the location, provenance or origin, and condition of museum collections are addressed by Service policy and data standards released in FY 1998. In an effort to assist field stations in managing their collections, the Service released a new museum property software package for tracking essential information and preparing annual reports. The Service estimates that it will require a minimum of eight years to identify and confirm its museum collections, 15 years to catalog 80 percent of the collections according to Department of the Interior standards, and at least 20 years to either improve storage conditions or consolidate collections in facilities that meet Departmental standards.

Special Designations

The Wilderness Protection Act of 1964 created the National Wilderness Preservation System. Designations ensure that lands in the Wilderness Preservation System are preserved and protected in their natural state. Wilderness is where the earth and its community of life are untrammeled by human beings and where humans themselves are visitors who do not remain. Of the approximately 90 million acres in the Wilderness Preservation System, the Service manages 75 wilderness areas encompassing 20.7 million acres in 26 States. This total represents approximately 23 percent of the National Wilderness Preservation System. These lands and resources are kept in their natural state and protected from man made disturbances and, as such, the condition of these lands is maintained so as to preserve the natural qualities for which they were originally designated. Although mostly located in the Western United States and Alaska, the Service manages a number of wilderness areas in the lower 48 States including those at Red Rock Lakes NWR in Montana and Monomoy Island NWR in Massachusetts.

The Red Rock Lakes NWR was established in 1935 to protect the rare trumpeter swan. One of the few marshland wilderness areas in the country, Red Rock Lakes NWR continues to be one of the most important habitats in North America for these majestic birds. Red Rock Lakes NWR is primarily a high elevation mountain wetland-riparian area. Red Rock Creek flows through the upper end of the Centennial Valley, within which the Refuge lies, creating the impressive Upper Red Rock Lake, River Marsh, and Lower Red Rock Lake marshlands. The rugged Centennial Mountains border the Refuge on the south, catching the snows of winter that replenish the refuge's lakes and marshes. Although much of the refuge lands were originally homesteaded at the turn of the century, much of the naturalness has been restored to the area and is managed for primitive wilderness values. This minimally-altered natural diversity provides habitat for other species such as sandhill cranes, curlews, peregrine falcons, eagles, numerous hawks and owls, badgers, wolverines, bears, and wolves (in the backcountry), native fish such as Arctic grayling and westslope cutthroat trout, moose, and pronghorn antelope. Formal trails are not maintained or designated. In keeping with the wilderness spirit, visitors are free to explore the country and follow numerous game trails, seeing the country the way wildlife see it, and follow in the trails and tracks of moose, elk, and deer.

Another example is the Monomoy NWR, located on the "elbow" of Cape Cod in Massachusetts. It stretches approximately 10 miles southward into the waters of Nantucket Sound and the

Monomoy South Island, Massachusetts

USFWS Photo

Atlantic Ocean. The 2,750-acre refuge was established in 1944 under the Migratory Bird Conservation Act for the protection of migratory waterfowl. The refuge boundary encompasses all of North and South Monomoy Islands and a 40-acre parcel of Morris Island, which is connected to the mainland by a causeway. In 1970, Congress designated 94 percent of the refuge as wilderness. It is the only wilderness area in southern New England.

North and South Monomoy Islands are classic barrier beach islands, with surf-battered dunes on the eastern shores that gradually flatten to salt marsh and

...and where humans themselves are visitors who do not remain.

Elise Smith/USFWS

Wilderness areas contribute significantly to the Service's primary mission and to...

Pat Heglund/USFWS

Service Employee in Alaska

an extensive area of shoals and mud flats on the western shore. Through the combined forces of storms and tides, the landscape of Monomoy NWR is in constant change. The Monomoy Islands were created when severe winter storms separated Monomoy Point from the mainland in 1958. Twenty years later, another storm severed North Monomoy Island from South Monomoy Island. Monomoy's isolated beach, dune, freshwater pond, and fresh- and salt-water marsh habitats support a variety of wildlife species. The refuge boasts the largest variety of breeding waterfowl species in the State, including mallard, northern pintail, American black duck, American widgeon, and blue-winged teal and provides nesting habitat for the threatened piping plover and endangered roseate tern. Monomoy's location along the Atlantic flyway makes it a major staging area for fall populations of migrating waterfowl, passerine, and shorebird species. Large numbers of sea ducks winter on the waters around Monomoy, and peregrine falcons and bald eagles pass through the refuge during migration. Gray and harbor seals use haulout sites on both North and South Monomoy Islands.

The Monomoy Wilderness includes North and South Monomoy Islands and is accessible only by ferry or private boat. The wilderness includes some of the most beautiful beaches in the Cape Cod region and offers outstanding opportunities for wildlife observation, nature study, recreational fishing, shellfishing, and hiking. Monomoy NWR

is considered one of the premier birdwatching spots in the eastern United States and fly-fishing on the Monomoy flats is rated world class in quality.

Information on wilderness areas is reported each year in the Service's Annual Report of Lands Under Control of the U.S. Fish and Wildlife Service. Wilderness areas contribute significantly to the Service's mission and to the purposes for which the NWRS was authorized by sustaining healthy ecosystems and wildlife habitat.

For a river to be eligible for the National Wild and Scenic Rivers System, it must be in a free flowing condition and it must possess one or more of the following specific values, such as scenic, recreational, geologic, fish and wildlife, historic, cultural, or other similarly unique characteristics. Eligibility studies are presented to Congress with a Presidential recommendation, where final designations are decided by Congress. There are 154 rivers containing 178 river segments included in the National Wild and Scenic River System and each mile designated is classified as wild, scenic, or recreational. The total system encompasses approximately 10,931 river miles of which the Service manages segments of eight Wild and Scenic Rivers totaling approximately 1,258 miles in length. These rivers are destined to run wild and free as long as they remain in the Wild and Scenic Rivers System and, as such, the condition of these lands and waters are maintained so as to preserve the natural qualities for which they were originally designated.

National Natural Landmarks (NNL) are management areas having national significance as sites that exemplify one of a natural region's characteristic biotic or geologic features. Sites must be one of the best-known examples of a unique feature and must be located in the United States or on the Continental Shelf. There are 587 designated natural landmarks throughout the United States, with 43 on units of the National Wildlife Refuge System encompassing about 3.5 million acres. Refuge landmarks vary from the meandering resacas of Laguna Atacosa in Texas, part of the Bayside Resaca Landmark, to the urban Tinicum Wildlife Preserve at John Heinz NWR in Pennsylvania.

An example is the Reelfoot Lake NNL located on the Reelfoot Lake NWR in

Tennessee. Reelfoot Lake includes cypress swamps, saw-grass jungles, water lily glades, and scattered bodies of open water formed in the winter of 1811-1812 as a result of the New Madrid earthquake, the most severe of any recorded in the United States. The NNL includes geological features created by the earthquake and its after-shocks.

Other Service-managed landmarks recognize important ecological or geological features deserving protection and further study. National Natural Landmarks are designated by the Secretary of the Interior because they possess characteristics of a particular type of natural feature, have not been seriously disturbed by humans, contain diverse or rare natural features, or possess outstanding scientific values and educational opportunities. Their condition is maintained and managed to preserve the natural qualities for which they were originally designated.

Adopted in 1971, in Ramsar, Iran, the Convention on Wetlands of International Importance provides a framework for the conservation of wetlands worldwide. Marsh, fen, peatland, or water, whether static or flowing; fresh, brackish or salt and riparian or coastal zones adjacent to wetlands are included in and protected by the Ramsar Convention, embraced by more than 100 nations throughout the world. Ramsar recognizes the special value of 775 Wetlands of International Importance located throughout 93 countries in the World. There are 20 refuges that encompass 17 United States RAMSAR sites. One example, the Quivira NWR in Kansas, was featured at the second annual United States RAMSAR meeting held in Great Bend, Kansas, in April 2001. The meeting included Cheyenne Bottoms, a State managed RAMSAR site and Quivira NWR. Both sites are crucial for many migratory bird species and the refuge and the State-managed area share management goals and opportunities. The refuge is an excellent example of an inland salt marsh, a rare habitat type within the region. In addition to millions of migratory birds, the refuge provides habitat for listed species including the bald eagle, peregrine falcon, interior least tern and piping plover. The marshes of Quivira NWR provide critical habitat for endangered

whooping cranes during both the fall and spring migrations.

The Western Hemisphere Shorebird Reserve Network (WHSRN) was created in 1986 to foster international shorebird conservation partnerships among countries throughout the Americas. Sites are accepted into the WHSRN if they satisfy biological criteria and all owners and stakeholders agree to make a commitment to shorebird conservation. The Service broadly supports the WHSRN. The NWRS boasts an enormous array of shorebird habitats. At present 21 sites are managed within the NWRS, nine of which hold international status. Sites range throughout the U.S. from Virginia's shores (Eastern Shore NWR) to the California coast (San Francisco Bay NWR). In 2001, the WHSRN Council approved three new regional sites. The addition of J. Clark Salyer NWR in North Dakota, Edwin B. Forsythe NWR in New Jersey and Kvichak Bay (not Service land) in Bristol Bay, Alaska, brings the total of partnerships to 187, and the number of shorebird habitat acres to 20 million. J. Clark Salyer NWR provides habitat for the endangered piping plover and other shorebird species like the American avocet, upland sandpiper and common snipe. E.B. Forsythe NWR is recognized as a top site for the black-belled plover, semipalmated sandpiper, dunlin and short-billed dowitcher. Official site designations for new and existing sites occurred at J. Clark Salyer, the Lake Erie marshes (including Ottawa NWR), and Laguna Atacosa NWR, Texas.

Boundary Posting

...the purposes for which the NWRS was authorized by helping to sustain healthy ecosystems and wildlife habitat.

Setting Decoys

Supplementary Information on Service Performance

The Year at a Glance

Meeting the challenges of providing and protecting a healthy environment for fish and wildlife and for people is central to the programs of the Service. Dedicated Americans, combined with our dedicated International partners, are sharing a common commitment to conservation and are working hand-in-hand with the Service to ensure that our Nation's irreplaceable natural heritage and international fish and wildlife resources are protected for the enjoyment of this and future generations.

Portions of this narrative reference specific program accomplishments achieved under the Service's mission goals identified in its revised Five-Year Strategic Plan. The Service selected one annual performance goal for each of its four mission goals to represent Service performance. A comprehensive report on all program achievements under each strategic and mission goal presented in the Service's Five-Year Strategic Plan can be found in the Service's budget documents and in the Service's FY 2001 Annual Performance Report. The Service has made progress in developing the essential processes that support data verification methods in determining data quality. The Service has standardized data definitions, identified data sources, and determined data reliability and validity for all goals and measures. Performance data for goals are obtained by existing data collection processes and are supported by program information management systems.

The Financial Statements and the annual accomplishments highlighted in this section entitled, "The Year at a Glance," are organized according to the Service's four mission goals. The Service chose a considered approach in building the budget-performance linkages in phases. As an initial step to integrate the Service's performance structure with the budget in FY 2001, the Service adopted a strategy of disaggregating budget program activities into component parts and applying performance goals and indicators to those parts. These reassembled groups are termed Government Performance and Results Act (GPRA) program activities and it is through the GPRA program activities that the Service delivers its mission and

the annual performance plan. Consistent with linking budgetary resources to GPRA program activities, the Service reflects the cost of performance in the Statement of Net Cost, as presented in the Principal Financial Statements that follow this discussion. Since performance is delivered through Service organizational entities, the Statement of Net Cost reflects costs of producing each GPRA program activity from each of the Service's primary organizational entities for delivering program performance, which serve as the Service's responsibility segments.

Sustainability of Fish and Wildlife Populations
Many of the Nation's and the world's native fish, wildlife and plant populations are declining or are at historic low levels due to habitat degradation, inadequate fish passage, overuse, poaching, illegal trade in wildlife and wildlife products, introductions of invasive or nonindigenous species, poor land management practices, or urbanization.

The Service and its cooperators and partners are showing results. Under Mission Goal 1, Sustainability of Fish and Wildlife Populations, and Strategic Goal 1.2 entitled, "Imperiled Species," the Service set a goal in FY 2001 to stabilize or improve 53 percent of or 328 of 616 threatened or endangered species populations listed for a decade or more. Also, the Service planned to delist three species due to recovery under the Endangered Species Act and targeted three species at risk for which listing could be precluded due to conservation agreements.

The Service achieved a level of 320 species stable or improving in FY 2001, falling short of its target of 328 species (this represents an increment of 11 whereas the target represents an increment of 19 above the FY 2000 level). There are several reasons why the Service fell short of its goal. First is the increasing difficulty and complexity of bringing species back from the brink of extinction. Service resources are directed toward the greatest recovery challenges. The increasing frequency and severity of water shortages due to development or drought pose especially difficult challenges for stabilization of

Whooping Crane, Patuxent NWR, MD

The Service seeks to protect fish, wildlife and plant resources to prevent their decline before...

Mussel

many aquatic species. Many wide-ranging species facing multiple threats also pose especially difficult challenges. Also, demand for greater stakeholder involvement in the recovery process has required additional resources and time. In addition, increasing litigation in the Recovery Program has required more resources to be directed toward litigation support.

The Service delisted one species in FY 2001 falling short of its target of three delistings. The Service failed to finalize two additional delistings, the Bald Eagle and the Douglas County population of the Columbian white-tailed deer, due to delays caused by unforeseen issues. For example, in the case of the Columbian white-tailed deer, additional information submitted during the public comment period for the proposed delisting necessitated additional analysis and a reopening of the comment period. Although the two expected delistings were not finalized in FY 2001, the Service expects to finalize these delistings in early FY 2002. The Service also expects to delist three additional species in FY 2002 thereby achieving the combined FY 2001 and FY 2002 delisting target of six species by the end of FY 2002.

Significant progress was made in delivering an expanded Section 6, Cooperative Endangered Species Conservation Fund (CESCF) Grants to States program. In FY 2001, $104 million was appropriated to the CESCF, representing an increase of approximately $82 million over the FY 2000 level. The Service continued to deliver the long-standing and highly successful $7.5 million Conservation Grants program for listed species habitat restoration, status surveys, captive propagation and reintroduction, and other essential activities. The Habitat Conservation Plan Land Acquisition Grants program, now in its fifth year, increased to almost $69 million and funded 15 acquisitions of valuable recovery habitats in 10 states, helping acquire vital habitat for threatened and endangered species ranging from loggerhead turtles in Florida to imperiled songbirds in Texas. The funds, distributed as part of the Service's Habitat Conservation Plan land acquisition program, paid up to 75 percent of the cost of 15 proposals in California, Florida, Georgia, Maryland, Montana, North Carolina, Texas, Utah, Washington, and Wisconsin. Non-Federal partners contributed at least 25 percent of the cost of each project. In

addition, the FY 2001 increase provided for the first-time funding of four new grant programs: $4.74 million for Safe Harbor Grants, $4.74 million for Candidate Conservation Agreement Grants, $6.635 million for HCP Planning Assistance Grants, and $10.427 million for Recovery Land Acquisition Grants.

Recovery planning and implementation staved off extinction of several species, such as the silvery minnow. The Service also brought many species closer to recovered status. For example, the delisting of the Aleutian Canada goose and the proposed delisting of the Hoover's woolly-star and Robbin's cinquefoil were finalized. Implementing recovery actions while increasing flexibility for landowners has also been a focus of the recovery program in FY 2001. The Service published four experimental population designation rules, with special rules to accommodate existing land uses, covering 23 species including the whooping crane, black-footed ferret, 16 mussels, one snail, and four fish.

This year 246 plant and animal species were candidates for listing. Additionally, some of the 39 species that are currently proposed for listing under the Endangered Species Act (ESA) can benefit from candidate conservation actions that reduce or eliminate the need to publish a final listing. For others, conservation actions taken before listing will assist in a speedier recovery and delisting. Also, conservation agreements made listing under the ESA unnecessary for five species, which exceeded the FY 2001 target of three species. Further, restoration plans and accompanying support analyses for the Nisqually NWR supported recovery and protection of threatened and endangered aquatic species and their habitats. With such actions, the Service opens new miles of stream habitat, previously blocked for fish passage, for imperiled salmon and steelhead and other fishery resources.

Baseline data is collected on contaminants in wildlife used for subsistence. For example, FY 2001 funds were used to collect data on declining populations of Chinook and chum salmon from two Alaskan sites (Yukon and Kuskokwim Rivers). A range of contaminants (including heavy metals and persistent organochlorines) and indicators of biological effects (including histology, numerous biomarkers, and fish health) are measured to evaluate the effects of contaminants on salmon health and populations. The Service is also cooperating with State and Tribal public health agencies to generate a human health risk assessment for subsistence consumers of these salmon.

In addition to freshwater and anadromous species, the Service emphasizes species conservation and protection for marine species. Pursuant to the Marine Mammal Protection Act (MMPA), the Service manages the northern sea otter in Alaska and Washington State, polar bear and Pacific walrus in Alaska, and supports efforts to recover the listed southern sea otter in California and the West Indian manatee in Florida and Puerto Rico. Marine mammal populations are protected and enhanced through enforcement, education, and outreach efforts by Service biologists.

The Service works closely with Russia on the management and conservation of polar bear populations. On October 16, 2000, the United States Assistant Secretary of State and the Russian Ambassador to the United States signed a landmark bilateral conservation and management agreement for the shared Alaska-Chukotka polar bear population. This agreement will allow substantial involvement by Alaska and Russia Native peoples and provide a unified, long-term, and scientifically based conservation for this population of polar bear.

The Service's Partners for Fish and Wildlife Program is a voluntary habitat restoration program that works with private landowners and Native American governments who are interested in restoring wetlands, prairies, streams and other important fish and wildlife habitats on their own lands. The program's philosophy is to work proactively with private landowners for the mutual benefit of declining Federal trust species and the landowners involved. Restoration projects include battling invasive exotic plant species and working to raise public understanding of the benefits of native plant and animal communities. These voluntary efforts by private landowners and Native American Tribes help to recover listed species and help to preclude the listing of rare or candidate species.

There are wildlife populations that are considered nuisances. Aquatic invasive species concern the Service and its Federal, State, and non-governmental partners. In FY 2001, 10 grants were provided to States and Tribes to help

Walrus in Alaska

prevent and control aquatic nuisance species. Specifically, the 100th Meridian Initiative, designed to stop the westward spread of zebra mussels and other aquatic invasive species, focuses on trailered boats as the primary pathway of introduction. The Service hosted a workshop during National Fishing Week with the goal of educating attendees about how the public may prevent the spread of nuisance species while still enjoying aquatic recreation, such as boating and fishing.

Through aggressive reduction plans and actions, the Service and its partners are addressing overabundance of mid-continent populations of light geese. High populations of geese result in accelerated habitat degradation and increased chances of major disease outbreaks, which are a threat to the geese themselves and other bird species. During most of the past 30 years, the winter index of mid-continent light geese increased from 900,000 birds to nearly 3,000,000 birds, because of increased availability of food on agricultural lands and a decline in overall mortality of birds. Recent population surveys of mid-continent light geese indicate some reduction in the overall population, which may be a direct result of the Service's implementation of Regional Snow Goose Action Plans in the Central and Mississippi Flyways and new regulations that allow increased harvest of light geese.

International partnerships to protect and conserve fish, wildlife and plants

...they need the special attention made possible under the Endangered Species Act.

throughout the world are as diverse as domestic partnerships forged to protect and conserve our Nation's resources. Global wildlife conservation relies on international cooperation, education and enforcement at all levels. Not only is the Service advising foreign governments, but also the Service is a catalyst for community conservation action at the individual and local level in foreign nations.

In 2001, the Service put money on the ground for Great Ape conservation and provided the first grant assistance under the Great Ape Conservation Act of 2000. A call for proposals to more than 100 African and Asian national governments and non-governmental organizations was answered with project proposals for gorillas, chimpanzees, bonobos, orangutans, and gibbons. For example, the Great Ape Conservation Fund provided support to the Orangutan Tropical Peatland Project to collect information on the orangutan population of the tropical peat swamp forests of southeast Central Kalimantan, Indonesia, and on threats to its integrity and survival. In addition, the Wildlife Conservation Society received a grant to conduct research and protection and management activities on a population of chimpanzees in the Goualougo Triangle in the northern Republic of Congo-Brazzaville. The bonobo received support through a grant to the Zoological Society of Milwaukee to equip and train ecoguards from the Institut Congolais pour la Conservation de la Nature (ICCN). Further, the African Wildlife Foundation received a grant to conduct an extensive ranger-based monitoring program in protected areas of the Virunga-Bwindi Forest Ecosystem, in Uganda, Rwanda, and the DRC. The Virunga-Bwindi Forest Ecosystem is the only home of the mountain gorilla, of which only approximately 650 individuals remain.

Habitat Conservation
Accomplishments in species conservation are intertwined with and, in many cases, dependent on the benefits associated with habitat conservation. Because fish and wildlife are mobile, habitat loss, degradation, and fragmentation are key factors affecting fish and wildlife populations. In this subsection, the Service highlights its work with its partners to protect, restore and manage priority habitats in sufficient quality and quantity for the benefit of fish, wildlife and plant species and the healthy

ecosystems upon which they depend for survival.

Under Mission Goal 2, Conserving Habitat Through a Network of Lands and Waters, and Strategic Goal 2.1 entitled, "Habitat Conservation on Service Lands," the Service set three goals this year to meet the identified habitat needs of Service lands. The first target was to ensure that 3,144,559 acres in the NWRS were managed and enhanced. The Service exceeded this goal this year by increasing the number of acres managed and enhanced in the NWRS to 3,358,893 acres. The second target was to restore 244,769 acres in the NWRS. The Service restored 105,601 acres, falling short of its target. The reason for the shortfall was due to erroneous data estimating in the North American Wetlands Conservation Program. This program has now been corrected with a new database and improved reporting procedures. The second goal was to add 255,000 acres to the NWRS over the previous year supporting fish and wildlife species population objectives. The Service exceeded this goal by adding more than 1.2 million acres to the NWRS in FY 2001. The third goal was to complete the development of standardized protocols to monitor the biological integrity, diversity, and environmental health of habitats in the NWRS. Although these protocols have not been developed in final form, a suite of standard biotic and abiotic data requirements for each refuge have been developed. They will become the baseline from which each refuge will monitor the biological integrity, biodiversity, and environmental health of national wildlife refuges. These standard requirements are currently in draft stage and will be incorporated into an update of Service Manual chapter on inventory and monitoring (701 FW 2) scheduled to be completed about July of 2002.

The Service will continue to have the NWRS and the NFHS serve as the examples for ecosystem stability in areas throughout the country and as critical tools to ecosystem and species recovery. But the Service recognizes that these systems cannot do the job alone.

Through the National Coastal Wetlands Conservation Grant Program, the Service provides resources to States to protect and restore coastal habitats. In FY 2001, the Service funded 22 projects giving 11 States approximately $15 million in matching grants for

Purple Prairie Clover

acquisition, restoration and enhancement of about 11,300 acres of coastal wetlands. In the State of Washington, for example, National Coastal Wetlands Conservation Grant funds will help the Department of Fish and Wildlife acquire 200 acres of wetland habitat and restore a total of 1,050 acres of estuarine wetlands of the lower Columbia River Estuary. This project, which is being accomplished with the help of Sea Resources and Ducks Unlimited, will provide high quality rearing and overwintering habitat for salmonids, including several species listed as threatened. It will also provide important habitat for migratory shorebirds, waterfowl and birds of prey.

The Partners for Fish and Wildlife Program works with private landowners to provide them with the knowledge and tools to improve the condition of fish and wildlife habitat on their land. In FY 2001, more than 3,000 private landowners were provided with technical and financial assistance and restored 48,800 acres of wetlands, 334,800 acres of grasslands, woodland, and scrub/shrub habitat, 800 miles of streamside habitat, and 190 miles of in-stream habitat. Also, more than 100 barriers to fish passage were removed and more than 300 miles of habitat to fish access were reopened. With additional funds this year, the Partners Program was able to combat invasive plant species on over 40,000 acres of private land. For example, in South Florida 12 projects were initiated to eradicate exotics from more than 400 acres of privately owned land. These projects will restore wildlife habitat and benefit threatened and endangered species such as the Wood stork, Florida panther, Audubon's crested caracara and Eastern indigo snake.

Also, the Partners Program assisted the White Mountain Apache Tribe of Arizona with aquatic habitat restoration work for the federally listed Apache trout and assisted the Hualapai Indian Tribe to restore imperiled desert springs which are important to their religion as well as to endemic fish species. In Wisconsin, the Partners Program is restoring the degraded oak savanna ecosystem that once dominated this region. Through selective tree cutting and prescribed fire, Karner Blue butterfly habitat is being restored. In California, the Service is working with local watershed groups to develop water quality plans. Project cooperators are managing for antelope, quail, sandhill cranes, neotropical

migratory songbirds, bald eagles, and the imperiled sage grouse.

Further, the Partner's Program uses funds to restore habitat for native cutthroat trout, bull trout, and grayling by removing fish barriers, screening irrigation diversions, creating off-channel livestock watering facilities, and fencing riparian corridors. In Pennsylvania, the Partner's Program is working with The Nature Conservancy to control invasive plants in their bog turtle habitat restoration program and with Northampton County to control common reed and purple loosestrife that had overtaken a series of calcareous fen communities containing several rare plant species and bog turtles.

Rio Grande Cutthroat Trout

Mountain Plover

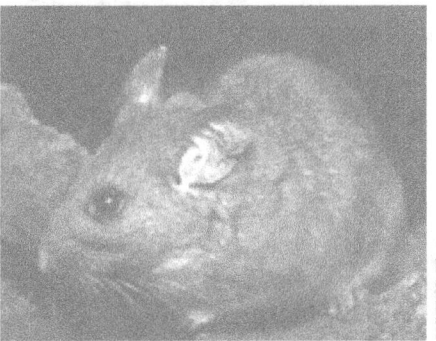
Riparian Woodrat

Polar Bear

The Coastal Program focuses its efforts on restoring and protecting coastal habitats on both private and public lands and is actively involved in projects in 14 high priority coastal watersheds that directly enhance the livability of coastal communities. In FY 2001, the Coastal Program restored 23,000 acres of coastal wetlands, 3,100 acres of upland habitats, and 180 miles of streamside habitat within coastal watersheds. Coastal Program projects removed seven barriers to fish passage, reopening 28 miles of fish habitat.

The ability to sustain ecosystems, and the natural heritage of fish, wildlife and plant resources within them...

Additional funding expanded the Florida Gulf Coastal Program, which is restoring unique habitats, such as dune and coastal lake shoreline areas, for rare and declining species such as piping plovers and the endangered beach mouse. The Coastal Program is also working with the Marine Institute to protect sea grass beds, which are winter feeding areas for Gulf of Mexico Sturgeon. The Service and the municipality of Panama City developed an alternative for the future removal of the City's treated effluent currently being discharged into the shellfish harvesting waters of West Bay (St. Andrew Bay). The project will restore wetlands altered by silviculture, help to assure long-term preservation of large cypress domes, provide habitat for numerous wetland-dependent species, and provide a wetland educational opportunity for the public.

The California Bay-Delta Program (CALFED) is a joint Federal-State effort to improve water management and restore the ecosystem of California's Sacramento-San Joaquin Delta Estuary and San Francisco Bay. The Service plays a key Federal role in all aspects of the development and implementation of the Program with special responsibilities for habitat restoration and species protection. Work in FY 2001 focused on tiered, regional planning for implementation of water supply, levee, and ecosystem improvements in the north and south Delta regions, continued implementation of ecosystem restoration projects, and improved management of the water supply system in the Delta.

Through the Middle Rio Grande (Bosque) program, the Service works with states, local entities and the Republic of Mexico to apply environmental conservation strategies along the southwestern U.S. border. The Service uses informal and formal efforts, such as binational agreements, to identify degradation of the border environment and to recommend and implement solutions.

Landscape approaches to conservation, whether at local-level sites or across continents, are essential to conserve important waterfowl habitat and wetlands. Since the inception of the North American Waterfowl Management Plan (NAWMP) in 1986, the Service has worked with regional, national and international partners to protect and restore habitat throughout the

continent for waterfowl and other wildlife that use wetlands. A host of diverse habitat protection and restoration projects are delivered through NAWMP partnerships. More than six million acres of essential and diverse habitat has been protected for the future. Congress noted this success with an increase of $2.2 million to the NAWMP partnerships in FY 2001. In the United States, there are currently 12 habitat and three species NAWMP partnerships. In association with the NAWMP partnerships, there are new "all-bird" conservation initiatives that are being launched in the Central Hardwoods, West Gulf Coastal Plain, Northern Great Plains, and Lower Great Lakes and St. Lawrence Valley. NAWMP partnerships are key to implementing the vision of the North American Bird Conservation Initiative, which calls for simultaneous on-the-ground delivery of conservation for all North American birds. A principal thrust will be to coordinate all existing and new bird conservation plans with the NAWMP. These existing plans include the United States Shorebird Conservation, North American Waterbird Conservation Plan, Partners in Flight, and a developing coalition of states for resident game bird conservation. Working with counterparts in Canada and Mexico, the Service is helping to prepare a non-binding agreement for international bird conservation and characteristics for outstanding international bird conservation projects.

Another key tool in protecting migratory birds and other wildlife habitat across the continent is the North American Wetlands Conservation Act (NAWCA). Funds appropriated for the NAWCA make up the largest component of the four funding sources of the North American Wetlands Conservation Fund. FY 2001 witnessed unprecedented support from Congress, with an appropriation of $40 million, an increase of $25 million over FY 2000. This

Table 1

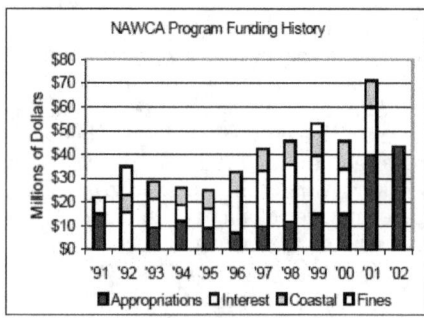

increase was met by an equally significant increase in partner support. With this strong support, nearly 610,000 acres were protected or restored, in 37 states, with more than $212.8 million in partner funds and $41.8 million in grant funds - a 5:1 ratio. In Canada, more than 781,000 acres were protected and enhanced, with more than $23.6 million in grant funds and $38.4 million in partner funds. Continued growth in the Mexican program was again demonstrated with 22 projects affecting almost 242,000 acres, with nearly $3.3 million in grant funds and more than $4.5 million in partner support. With continued support from Congress, important strides will continue to be made in the conservation of migratory birds.

Linking Wildlife and People
The ability to sustain ecosystems, and the natural heritage of fish, wildlife and plant resources within them, will increasingly depend on the public's active participation in the stewardship of these valuable resources. A growing number of the public lacks first-hand experience with fish and wildlife resources in their natural setting. Thus, the Service provides environmental education to help the public understand how their well-being is linked to the well-being of fish, wildlife and plant resources. Also, private citizens, whose voluntary participation in fish and wildlife conservation, laid a foundation on which the Service operates today and have contributed to the continuing conservation of fish and wildlife resources throughout the world.

New community-based Friends Groups and other volunteer refuge support groups are being developed on a continuing basis nationwide. Groups consist of local citizens who have established community partnerships supporting the mission of their hometown national wildlife refuge. Because group memberships are derived from private citizens in communities across the nation, the NWRS is supported by a growing constituency, which reflects a rich diversity of wildlife conservation interests. This wealth of ideas, skills, talents, and expertise being woven into friends groups will both strengthen and enrich the NWRS.

Mission Goal Three recognizes the public benefit that Americans enjoy from experiencing fish, wildlife and their habitat. Under strategic goal 3.2 entitled, "Opportunities for Participating in Conservation on Service Lands," the Service set two goals, the first to increase volunteer participation hours in Service programs by two percent and the second to foster 108 new friends groups for a total of 171. The first performance measure was not met. The target was 1,360,000 hours; the estimated final value was 1,267,830 hours, or 93 percent of the target. The number of volunteers that can be accommodated may be near the saturation point. Lack of staff time to nurture and develop volunteer programs may be the cause of this stabilization. The NWRS and the NFHS are presently understaffed by professional resource managers and are unable to redirect current refuge staff time to provide additional support to the volunteer program without adversely impacting resource management responsibilities on Service lands. The second performance measure was not met. The target was 171 new friends groups; the final number was 149, or 87 percent of the target. The long-term goal for adding friends groups is likely overly optimistic and will be revised. Large increases in the number of friends groups are diminishing as groups are already in place at larger, more heavily visited refuges. Remaining refuges are less likely to attract sufficient interest to form these officially organized support groups. Further, it is very difficult for smaller refuges and fish hatcheries, which do not have the necessary personnel to organize and support the considerable administrative tasks associated with managing these groups. Citizens at smaller more remote refuge field stations are volunteering as individuals rather than establishing a larger support organization.

An important planning and conservation tool made available to our public and private partners is the ability to locate existing wetlands and other habitat significant to the conservation of fish and wildlife resources. A significant role of the Service's National Wetlands Inventory is to provide the public with wetlands data that can be used by decision makers to support conservation of wetlands and other aquatic habitats. In January 2001, the Service released its report, *Status and Trends of Wetlands in the Conterminous United States 1986 to 1997*. This Congressionally-mandated report indicated that the Nation lost an estimated 58,500 acres of wetlands annually during 1986 to 1997. This is the greatest measured overall decline in the rate of wetland loss since the Federal Government began compiling records.

Night-lighting crew

J. Gulke/USFWS

...will increasingly depend on the public's active participation in the stewardship of these valuable resources.

The Service supports and strengthens partnerships with State and local governments, tribal governments and with the purpose of conserving fish, wildlife, plants and their habitats.

These results highlight the need for the American public to remain diligent in its commitment to wetland protection so the progress being made in stemming the loss of this precious resource is not lost in the future.

Partnerships in Natural Resources
The Service supports and strengthens partnerships with State and local governments, tribal governments and with the purpose of conserving fish, wildlife, plants and their habitats. We build on common interest and values to achieve the greatest possible benefits for natural resources.

State and Territorial agencies are integral to the successful conservation of fish and wildlife resources. Grant programs assisting States and Territories provide effective delivery and tracking of grants. Under Mission Goal 4, "Partnerships in Natural Resources," and Strategic Goal 4.2 entitled, "Sport Fish and Wildlife Restoration Grants Management," the Service set a goal to improve grant management by increasing the number of Federal Aid program staff trained in modern grant management processing, specifically including the use of the Federal Aid Information Management System (FAIMS). Also, the Service strived to complete 95 percent of phase 1 implementation of FAIMS. Both these goals were met. The Division of Federal Aid trained 20 employees in the use of FAIMS. This included two formal workshops for Regional staff and a briefing for Regional Office managers in the use and maintenance of this system. One ad hoc training session was also provided to satisfy a specific Regional Office request to help orient a newly recruited fiscal specialist. The FAIMS implementation is nearing completion. This year the system was 95 percent complete, lacking only a web interface for client interaction with the system. Future efforts will be toward establishing this interface and cooperative efforts with other agencies in the Department toward an automated grants management system.

The Service's Federal Aid in Sport Fish Restoration and the Federal Aid in Wildlife Restoration Programs are the mainstays of State fish and wildlife resource management efforts. Excise taxes, collected from manufacturers of equipment used in hunting and fishing, shooting ranges, and on motorboat fuels, are deposited into a trust fund and

Treasury account for investment and then, after appropriate deductions, are apportioned to each State. The last five-year average apportionment to the States is more than $176 million for wildlife and more than $247 million for sport fish restoration. Also in FY 2001, $8 million was made available for the National Outreach and Communications Program authorized by the Transportation Equity Act for the 21st Century enacted in 1998. This law provides the 30 million anglers and 78 million boaters of America with additional resources through FY 2003 for sport fisheries management and restoration. This is not a gift from Congress, but rather is the model "user-pays, user-benefits" program. Users contribute through revenues collected from motorboat and small engine fuels taxes and excise taxes on fishing tackle, electric trolling motors, flasher-type sonar fish finders, and import duties on fishing tackle and pleasure boats.

During FY 2001, the Service began its implementation of the Federal Aid Improvement Act of 2000, and administrative funds were expended as specified in the Act. Implementation of the new Section 10 Hunter Education portion of the Act resulted in an early final apportionment of these one-year funds, new accounting codes to track them, and a policy for their expenditure. The Multistate Conservation Grant Program resulted in almost $6 million granted in FY 2001 to entities recommended by the International Association of Fish and Wildlife Agencies. The Supplementary Stewardship Information Section presents more information on grants awarded to States under the Service's Federal Aid Program.

The Service has a proud tradition of working with its partners throughout the Nation and the world to effect solutions that benefit fish and wildlife resources and the habitat upon which they depend for survival. The Service has enjoyed the increasing support of the Congress, the President, and the American public. We look forward to continuing to build new and nurture existing cooperative programs so that fish and wildlife management remains a useful and productive tool in conserving our valued fish and wildlife resources for future generations.

Facilities Management
In order to understand the condition of Service facilities, the Service estimates

deferred maintenance needs for the facilities and infrastructure that support the mission work of the Service. Annually, the Service must defer needed maintenance because of inadequately funded growth of the infrastructure without commensurate growth in operations and maintenance funding and competition for resources from other management needs. Having to defer repairs, rehabilitation or replacement of facilities and the physical resources fixed to facilities leads to accelerated facility deterioration. Such deterioration of facilities can adversely impact public and employee health and safety, disrupt operations of the Service, and compromise the conservation of fish and wildlife resources.

Refuge water management facilities, fish hatcheries, visitor centers, buildings, roads, dikes, dams, bridges, and other facilities represent a major investment by the American people in resources that support the mission of the Service. The deferred maintenance estimate for facilities in the NWRS is approximately $663 million, plus or minus 15 percent, placing the estimate within a range of approximately $564 million to $763 million. The deferred maintenance estimate for facilities within the NFHS is approximately $328 million, plus or minus 15 percent, placing the estimate within a range of approximately $279 million to $377 million. Deferred maintenance for aggregate facilities within both systems is estimated at approximately $991 million, plus or minus 15 percent, placing the range between approximately $843 million and $1.14 billion for all facilities under the jurisdiction of the Service. Estimating deferred maintenance requires the professional judgment of numerous site managers gathering information from multiple sources. These estimates can represent average costs among several sources or the last estimate increased over time to accommodate inflation. Each method is acceptable; however, estimates may vary by 15 percent above or below any discrete number provided.

The Service's estimates of deferred maintenance are aggregate estimates for all facilities and for all property related to facility operations. The aggregate estimates do not include construction of facilities not previously existing, significant expansion of existing facilities, or major upgrades of structures, but rather are estimates of bringing existing facilities into a functional or acceptable

operating condition. Maintenance of a minor, custodial nature, including grass mowing, snow removal, grounds maintenance, routine equipment servicing (excluding preventive maintenance), and janitorial services are not included in the Service's estimate. Equipment replacement is also excluded from this estimate.

A standard measure of condition for facilities is a ratio of the estimates of deferred maintenance needs to the replacement value of such facilities, known as the Facilities Condition Index (FCI). Estimates of deferred maintenance needs represent those field station maintenance needs that have not been funded for at least one year. The replacement value is the estimate for replacing these facilities at today's costs. The FCI illustrates the percentage of its capital amount that an institution would have to spend to eliminate the deferred maintenance. If the ratio of accumulated deferred maintenance to replacement value is from zero to five percent, the condition of the facilities is considered as "good." If the ratio is greater than five but less than 10 percent, the condition is considered as "fair" and if the ratio is 10 percent or greater, then condition is considered "poor." The replacement value for facilities within the NWRS is estimated at $7.2 billion and for the NFHS at $899 million, with a combined total of more than $8.1 billion. Based on condition assessment surveys conducted by the Service, the FCI for facilities within the NWRS is estimated at approximately 9.2 percent and for the NFHS at approximately 36.5 percent, with a combined FCI for all Service facilities estimated at approximately 12 percent. Therefore, the overall condition of Service facilities is "poor." A one-time funding initiative of approximately $991 million would be required to raise the condition of Service operating assets from poor to good. Based on the replacement estimates for existing facilities, the Service would require an annual maintenance budget higher than current or projected levels to maintain these assets in fair or good condition.

The Service estimates the total replacement value of Service operating assets to be at approximately $8.1 billion. Private sector or industry standards suggest that no less than two percent to four percent of the total replacement value of the asset should be expended annually for proper maintenance. Under this guideline, the Service would require

The Service has a proud tradition of working with its partners throughout the Nation and the world to effect solutions that benefit fish and wildlife resources and the habitat upon which they depend for survival.

an annual maintenance budget of at least $165 million in order to properly maintain the existing infrastructure of the NWRS and the NFHS. New additions to Service infrastructure will require commensurate increases to the maintenance budget of the Service to prevent increases in deferred maintenance.

Equipment Replacement and Repair
Although the estimates for deferred maintenance exclude associated equipment, the Service is tracking equipment needs in much the same manner as it tracks facility condition and maintenance. Equipment includes replacement or repair of non-fixed or portable physical resources (e.g., heavy equipment, transportation equipment and vehicles, small portable tools, computers and office equipment, and shop, lab, security, communications or other operational equipment). The Service tracks equipment that needs repair, rehabilitation, or replacement to bring it up to acceptable operating condition necessary for the Service to complete its mission and to conserve resources for which the Service has stewardship responsibility. The Service has determined that much of its equipment is in poor condition and, thus, in need of repair, rehabilitation or replacement.

Estimating the equipment backlog for the NWRS and the NFHS requires specifying equipment parameters and seeking competitive prices among differing vendors. As such, estimates may vary by 10 percent above or below the discrete number provided. However, the Service uses the median number within the range as the best estimate of the existing equipment backlog. The median estimate for equipment for the NWRS is approximately $355 million and for the NFHS is approximately $27 million, with a combined total of approximately $382 million. A one-time funding initiative of $382 million would be required to raise the condition of Service operating equipment assets from poor to an acceptable operating condition. Based on historical trends in annual maintenance budgets, the Service would require higher than current projected funds to maintain these assets in acceptable operating condition. The equipment backlog is an estimate of replacement cost. Private sector or industry standards suggest that no less

than two percent to four percent of the total replacement value of the asset should be expended annually for proper maintenance. Under this guideline, the Service would require an annual equipment maintenance budget of at least $7.7 million in order to properly maintain equipment managed by the Service. New additions to Service equipment and staff will require commensurate increases to the maintenance budget of the Service to prevent increases to the equipment replacement and repair backlog. The NWRS is initiating a new effort to annually replace a proportion of the total equipment fleet based on equipment, age, mileage, utilization, and program needs. The current inventory includes 7,225 items more than $5,000 in value with a total replacement cost of $355 million.

Management Controls and Legal Compliance

The Service is dedicated to maintaining the integrity and accountability in all programs and operations. Management assesses its systems of management, administrative and financial controls to ensure that:
- programs achieve their intended results;
- resources are used consistent with the Service's mission;
- resources are protected from waste, fraud and mismanagement;
- laws and regulations are followed; and,
- reliable and timely information is maintained, reported, and used for decision-making.

The Service assesses the adequacy of its management controls through continuous monitoring and periodic evaluations, consistent with Office of Management and Budget Circular A-123 and the Federal Managers' Financial Integrity Act. Each year, the Service identifies specific management control assessments planned for the fiscal year. The results from these internal reviews, as well as results in certain final audit reports issued primarily by the Office of Inspector General and the U.S. General Accounting Office are considered in the development of the Service's annual assurance statement on management controls. The statement also considers information obtained from the knowledge and experience management gained from the daily operation of programs and systems of accounting and administrative

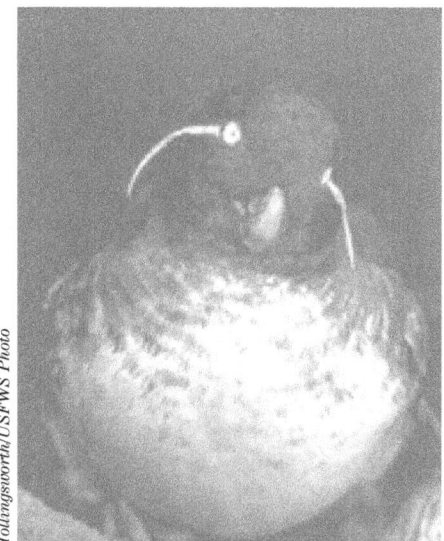

Parakeet Auklet, Alaska Maritime NWR

controls. The statement informs the Department of the effectiveness of the Service's management controls, and includes information about any pending and new Service-only material weaknesses and corrective actions.

In FY 2001, management control reviews were conducted in acquisition management (convenience checks), personal property management, and general support systems in information resources management, in the Duck Stamp Program, and in North American Wetlands Conservation Act grant activities. Twenty non-material control weaknesses were identified with corresponding planned corrective actions and planned completion dates in FY 2002 and FY 2003. Corrective actions are monitored until completion.

Service Performance Trends
Expected Changes in the Work of the Service
While the mission of the Service is unlikely to change significantly in the next five years, either in content or direction, emphasis in community and public outreach, public use and awareness, improved customer service, and improved technologies will certainly increase. The work performed by the Service will include an ever-increasing reliance on partnerships and cooperation with stakeholders as outlined in Secretary Norton's statements in support of the four C's (consultation, cooperation, communication – all in the service of conservation).

The Service is conducting an integrated set of studies on work force planning, strategic management of human capital, and functions and responsibilities of regional offices. Preliminary studies performed in FY 2001 will contribute to the integrated set of studies which will determine whether there will be a need for more expertise in data management and interactive data base systems (with Internet linkages). Service biologists are relying more on geographic information systems to accomplish mission activities. Budget, Finance, Administration, and Human Resources, whose work volume is affected by changes to all other programs and their data bases, will be on the cutting edge in developing new technological tools to integrate financial and program management processes. These include rolling out the Interior

Department Electronic Acquisition System (IDEAS), a revised personnel and payroll system (FHRIS), and new interfaces designed to transfer or incorporate program data into the core financial system and to integrate financial and program management.

Improving Delivery of Services
The Service is finding new ways to move services closer to the public by providing e-commerce for contracting purposes, web-based systems for customer services, and increasing technical assistance to citizens. The Service has made progress in improving the availability of information through the worldwide web and hosts more than 20,000 web pages of information on its field stations and activities. In addition to scientific and technical information, the Service web site provides the public with directories of Service offices and programs; visitor information for national wildlife refuges; news releases from the present back to 1914; information for vendors who want to bid on Service contracts; environmental education and homework help for students and teachers; lists of endangered species and available assistance grants; information on obtaining wildlife permits; and, career information and vacancies. Also, the Service is scanning and posting its extensive library of public domain photos so that these will be available to the public for downloading over the Internet, thereby reducing costs to the Service for fulfilling public requests for these materials. Further, the Service is creating a "virtual" library of its publications.

James C. Leupold/USFWS Photo

Marmot

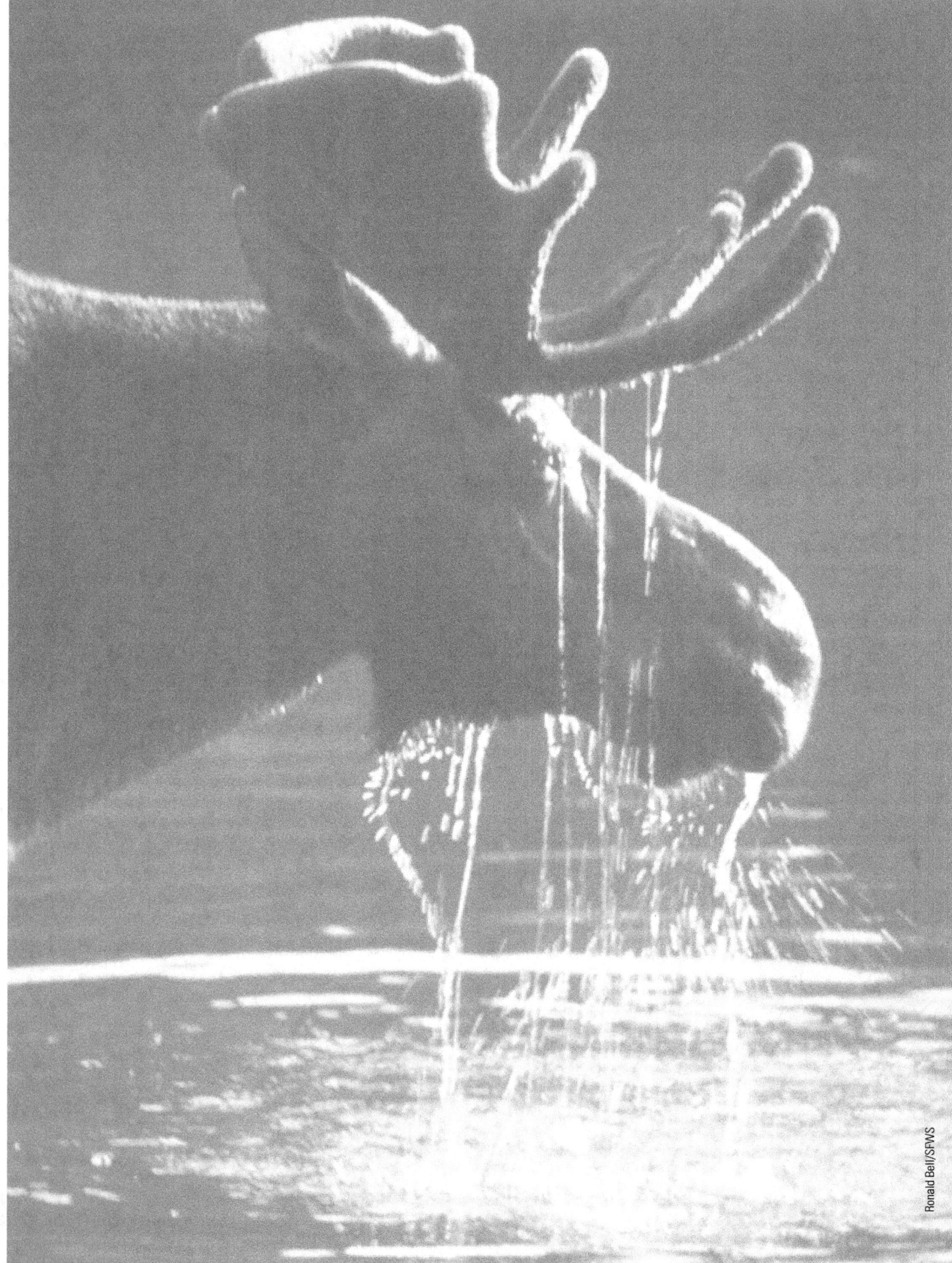

Service Financial Performance
*Message from the
Chief Financial Officer*

I am pleased to present the Service's audited financial statements for fiscal year 2001. These statements and the accompanying narrative provide the Congress and the public with a clear and comprehensive view of our achievements.

We met many new challenges this year and made significant management improvements to further integrate our financial and program management performance. Although we still have much to accomplish, our successes to date demonstrate our improved financial transaction, cost recovery and cost allocation processes. Improvements in these areas are significant steps in achieving the long-term accountability goals we have set for ourselves.

The Office of Inspector General and Department's auditing firm, KPMG LLP, played important roles in assisting us with accountability and process improvement through annual audits of our financial statements. The recommendations and opinions highlighted by these audits allowed us to focus on where we have been, what progress we have made, and where we need to go to further integrate financial and program management performance.

I appreciate the work of all those who helped us maintain quality financial statements. This achievement is the result of a tremendous effort from individuals at all levels of the Service.

I look forward to meeting the many challenges in the future.

Paul W. Henne
Chief Financial Officer
U.S. Fish & Wildlife Service

Financial Highlights

Reporting the Aquatic Resources Trust Fund on this Year's Financial Statements

The Service's Sport Fish Restoration Account (SFRA) makes grants available to States for support projects that restore, conserve, manage, protect, and enhance sport fish resources and coastal wetlands, and also for projects that provide for public use and benefits from sport fish resources. The source of funding for the SFRA is the Aquatic Resources Trust Fund (ARTF), which receives revenues through excise taxes levied on the sale of fishing tackle and equipment, certain motorboat and small engine gasoline, and interest earned on invested trust funds. In addition to the SFRA, the ARTF funds the Boating Safety Account, which provides funding for boating safety programs conducted by the U.S. Coast Guard, and also coastal wetlands initiatives conducted by the Corps of Engineers. Title 26 of the U.S. Code, Section 9602 designates the Department of the Treasury as manager of the ARTF, with overall responsibility for the fund's accounting and investment activities. This year, the ARTF is presented on the Service's financial statements in accordance with the requirements of Statement of Federal Financial Accounting Standard Number 7, Accounting for Revenue and Other Financing Sources, and Statement of Federal Financial Accounting Concepts Number 2, Entity and Display, which requires trust funds that finance multiple programs to be reported by the entity with the preponderance of fund activity. In FY 2001, the SFRA received approximately 79% of the ARTF transfers.

Environmental Cleanup Liabilities

In the footnote to the Financial Statements estimating environmental cleanup liabilities, the Service does not estimate the costs of restoring stewardship values or fish and wildlife resources that are degraded by offsite activities beyond the control of the Service. Excluding such costs from this footnote is required by Technical Release No. 2 of the Accounting and Auditing Policy Committee established to interpret standards set by the Federal Accounting Standards Advisory Board. The Service will pursue all administrative and legal means to seek compensation from polluters responsible for contaminating natural resources;

however, most cases pursued are usually settled out of court. The court usually awards less than the estimated value of the damages to fish and wildlife resources. Therefore, restoration does not fully compensate the American public for lost or damaged natural resources in affected units of the NWRS and the NFHS. After exhausting all legal and administrative remedies, the Service uses available operations and maintenance funds to cleanup residual contaminants and to restore habitat.

Service Financial Performance

In FY 2001 the Service improved financial management processes governing the performance of financial transactions and cost recovery and cost allocations. The Service is processing payments more efficiently and has improved its rate of compliance with Departmental and Federal payment processing requirements. During FY 2001, the Service addressed the necessary funding and accounting of its General Operations costs through full cost recovery from reimbursable partners and the equitable allocation of administrative support costs using the Cost Allocation Methodology.

Improving Financial Transaction Processes and Results

Throughout FY 2001, the Service's Chief Financial Officer (CFO) emphasized the need to strengthen financial transaction processes and improve compliance with federal and Department of the Interior performance targets. Accordingly, a monthly reporting system to monitor the Service's financial transaction processes was implemented. These monthly reports monitor Servicewide performance in the areas of prompt payment, electronic funds transfer, and credit card delinquencies. The reports are prepared directly for the Service's CFO and members of the Service Directorate. In each of the monitored transaction areas, the Service significantly improved its performance since the advent of this reporting program. Follow-up actions for lagging performance are coordinated at a national level by the CFO.

For FY 2001, the Service's prompt payment performance improved over the performance levels of prior years. As demonstrated in Figure 1, the Service made prompt payments at a 97.6 percent rate and paid a total of $88,419 in late

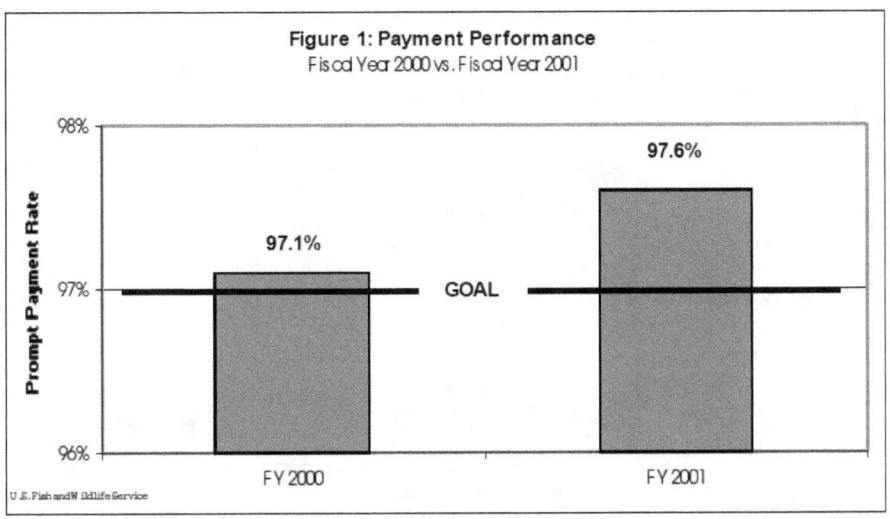

Figure 1: Payment Performance
Fiscal Year 2000 vs. Fiscal Year 2001

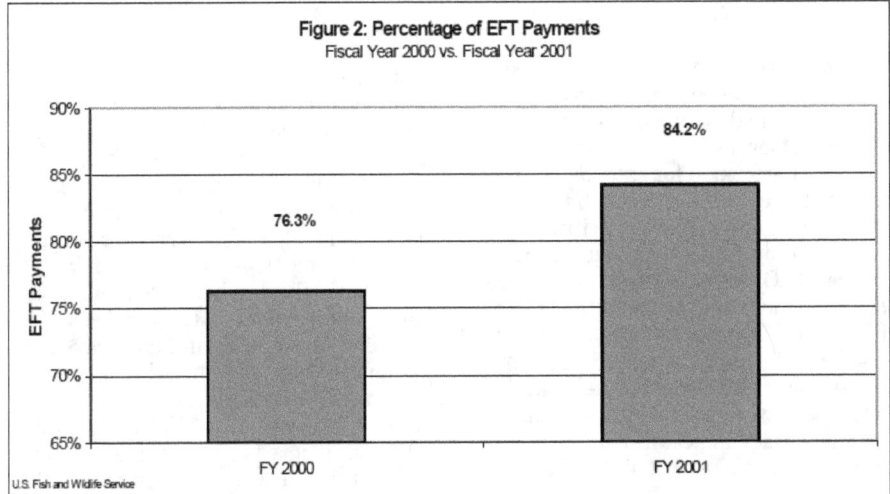

Figure 2: Percentage of EFT Payments
Fiscal Year 2000 vs. Fiscal Year 2001

payment penalties during FY 2001. This contrasts with the 97.1 percent rate of FY 2000.

Similar progress was made for electronic funds transfer payments (EFT). Figure 2 displays that in FY 2001, 84.2 percent of the Service's payments were accomplished through EFT. This is an improvement over the 76.3 percent rate achieved during FY 2000.

In response to Departmental efforts to minimize employee delinquencies in credit card payments outstanding for more than 60 days, this year the Service closely monitored its performance in this area. Reports on delinquencies were prepared for the CFO and the Service Directorate. These efforts proved successful, as the Service had one of the lowest delinquency rates within the Department. Figure 3 indicates that the Service had only 2.5 percent of its credit card balance outstanding and delinquent at the end of FY 2001. This compares favorably to the Departmental delinquency average of 5.4 percent and the Federal Government as a whole.

Improving Cost Recovery and Cost Allocation Practices
General Operations is the budgetary designation for the Service's national and Regional executive management Offices, administrative support functions, and key fixed operating costs. The Service relies on cost recovery and cost allocation to fully fund and account for these costs.

At the beginning of FY 2001, the Service implemented new policies to improve cost recovery and allocation of General Operations funding. The impetus for

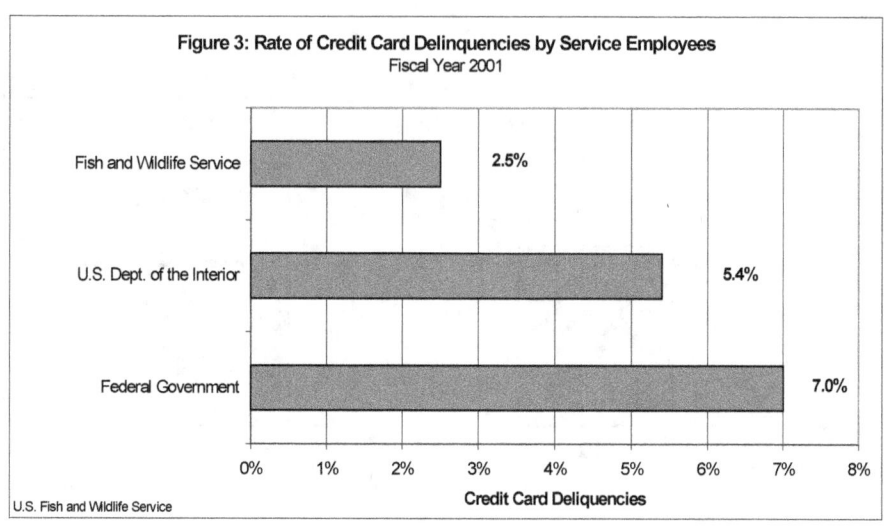

Figure 3: Rate of Credit Card Delinquencies by Service Employees
Fiscal Year 2001

U.S. Fish and Wildlife Service

change originated with an internal policy review that revealed the Service historically had not adequately recovered General Operations costs on work projects performed for external partners and customers on a cost reimbursable basis. In addition, audit activities conducted by the General Accounting Office (GAO) indicated that the Service disproportionately allocated the bulk of its General Operations costs to a small portion of its appropriated and receipt programs. GAO also indicated that these allocations were not tied to servicing levels or usage indicators, but rather were based on a program's "ability to pay."

To improve the recovery of General Operations costs from reimbursable work, the Service overhauled its national cost recovery policy, restructured its indirect cost rate structure and eliminated policy provisions that allowed indirect cost recovery to be waived by the Regional Directorate. These changes have resulted in a significant increase in the total amount of costs recovered for General Operations as well as a notable decrease in the number of reimbursable agreements exempted from indirect cost recovery. As depicted in Figure 4, $6.56 million was recovered in indirect costs associated with reimbursable work in FY 2001, an increase of $1.172 million over FY 2000. There is strong evidence that this increase relates to a reduction in the number of reimbursable agreements either receiving an exemption or meeting policy requirements to waive indirect costs.

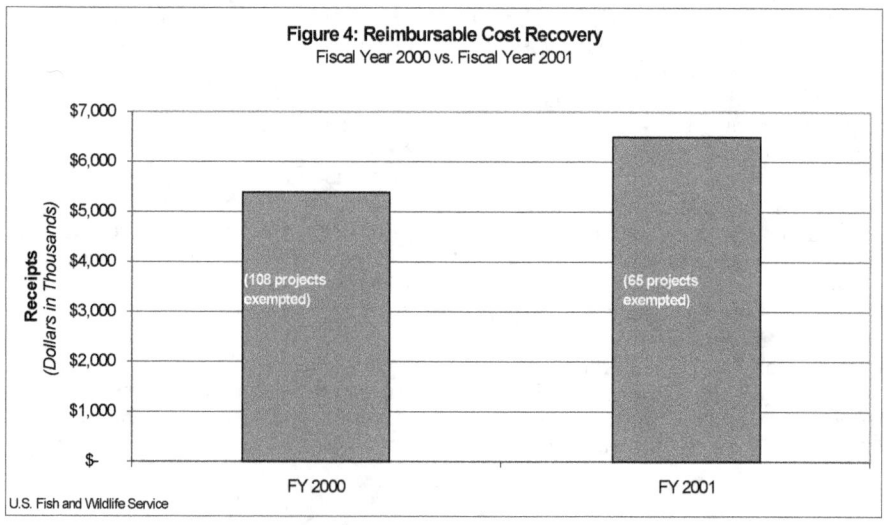

Figure 4: Reimbursable Cost Recovery
Fiscal Year 2000 vs. Fiscal Year 2001

U.S. Fish and Wildlife Service

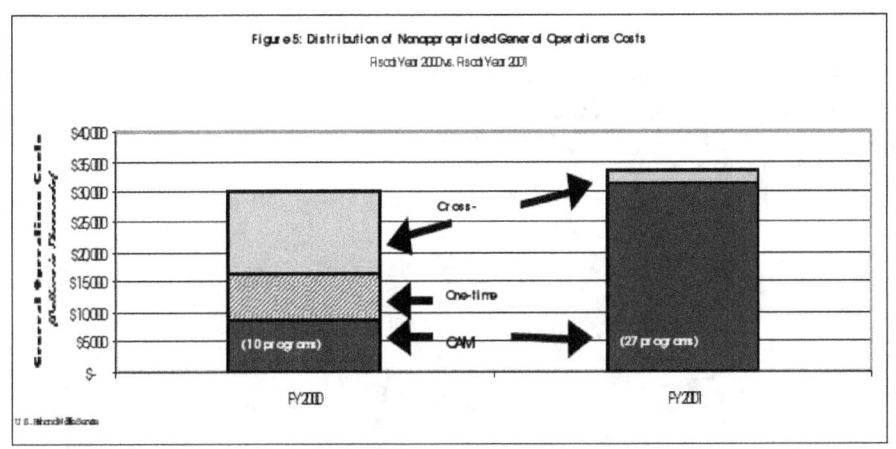

Figure 5: Distribution of Nonappropriated General Operations Costs
Fiscal Year 2000 vs. Fiscal Year 2001

At the end of FY 2000, the Service implemented the Cost Allocation Methodology (CAM) to promote the complete and equitable allocation of General Operations costs among its programs. The CAM centralizes all General Operations costs into a single cost pool and allocates these costs to all Service programs using specific cost drivers that track to usage and servicing levels. In FY 2001, $33.281 million in General Operations costs were allocated to 27 programs using usage/service-based cost drivers. This is a marked increase from FY 2000, in which the Service allocated $8.496 million to 10 programs and a dramatic improvement from FY 1999, in which $7.214 million was allocated to the same 10 programs based largely on the "ability to pay." Figure 5 displays that in previous years the difference was recovered by Congressional reprogramming and a large amount of administrative support costs charged directly to programs.

Two benefits of the changed policies are better identification of costs to Service programs and the creation of incentives for improved management. Assigning costs to programs directly has resulted in a substantial decrease in cross-charging

making it easier to understand the actual costs of operating Service programs and organizations. Using cost drivers based on actual usage allows managers the flexibility to attain savings for their respective programs by controlling the usage of said cost drivers. For example, reductions in the square footage of leased space occupied by a program (cost driver) will result in a cost savings to the program.

Limitations of the Financial Statements

The Principal Financial Statements that follow have been prepared to report the financial position and results of operations of the Service, pursuant to the requirements of 31.U.S.C. 3515(b). The statements have been prepared from the books and records of the Service in accordance with prescribed formats. The statements are different from the financial reports used to monitor and control budgetary resources, which are prepared from the same books and records. The financial statements should be read with the realization that they are a component of the U.S. Government, a sovereign entity, and that liabilities reported in the financial statements cannot be liquidated without legislation providing resources to do so.

Principal Financial Statements

U.S. Fish and Wildlife Service
CONSOLIDATED BALANCE SHEETS
As of September 30, 2001 and 2000
(dollars in thousands)

Assets		2001		Restated 2000 (Note 16)
Intragovernmental:				
Fund Balance with Treasury (Note 3)	$	1,194,342	$	907,497
Investments - Treasury Securities, Net (Note 5)		1,772,056		1,597,675
Accounts and Taxes Receivable, Net (Note 6)		28,696		47,917
Interest Receivable (Note 6)		4,791		3,270
Advances		2,055		866
Total Intragovernmental		3,001,940		2,557,225
Cash (Note 4)		140		458
Accounts and Taxes Receivable, Net (Note 6)		7,442		4,988
Interest Receivable, Net (Note 6)		55		47
Property, Plant, and Equipment, Net (Note 7)		783,115		758,355
Advances		663		585
Total Assets	$	3,793,355	$	3,321,658
Liabilities				
Intragovernmental:				
Accounts Payable	$	11,180	$	13,674
Accrued Payroll and Benefits		6,171		5,808
Unfunded FECA Liability (Note 9)		10,151		9,069
Advances from Others		26,196		2,835
Other Deferred Revenue		13,180		59,902
Payable for Invested Balances (Note 15)		335,416		299,258
Total Intragovernmental		402,294		390,546
Accounts Payable		81,192		70,145
Accrued Payroll and Benefits		24,290		22,952
Unfunded Annual Leave (Note 9)		37,153		35,827
Advances from Others		3,261		1,793
Actuarial FECA Liability (Note 9)		52,882		51,949
Environmental Clean-Up Liabilities (Notes 9 and 10)		46,807		42,000
Total Liabilities	$	647,879	$	615,212
Net Position				
Unexpended Appropriations (Note 13)		466,047		380,545
Cumulative Results of Operations		2,679,429		2,325,901
Total Net Position		3,145,476		2,706,446
Total Liabilities and Net Position	$	3,793,355	$	3,321,658

The accompanying notes are an integral part of these financial statements.

U.S. Fish and Wildlife Service
CONSOLIDATED STATEMENTS OF NET COST
For the years ended September 30, 2001 and 2000
(dollars in thousands)

	2001	Unaudited 2000
Sustainability of Fish and Wildlife Populations		
Gross Cost	$ 598,079	$ 596,681
Earned Revenue	49,371	40,903
Net Cost	548,708	555,778
Habitat Conservation: A Network of Land and Water		
Gross Cost	1,028,818	933,941
Earned Revenue	84,924	82,589
Net Cost	943,894	851,352
Public Use and Enjoyment		
Gross Cost	161,448	180,321
Earned Revenue	11,278	11,898
Net Cost	150,170	168,423
Partnerships in Natural Resources		
Gross Cost	3,445	-
Earned Revenue	33	-
Net Cost	3,412	-
Eliminations and Other		
Gross Cost	(584)	(519)
Earned Revenue	(584)	(625)
Net Cost	-	106
Totals		
Gross Cost	1,791,206	1,710,424
Earned Revenue	145,022	134,765
Net Cost of Operations (Note 18)	$ 1,646,184	$ 1,575,659

The accompanying notes are an integral part of these financial statements.

U.S. Fish and Wildlife Service
CONSOLIDATED STATEMENT OF CHANGES IN NET POSITION
For the year ended September 30, 2001
(dollars in thousands)

Net Cost of Operations	$	(1,646,184)
Financing Sources		
Appropriations Used		992,733
Tax Revenue		613,428
Other Financing Sources		30,003
Interest		98,070
Non-Exchange Revenue		8,394
Imputed Financing Sources (Note 14)		33,084
Transfers, Net		224,000
Total Financing Sources		1,999,712
Net Results of Operations		353,528
Increase In Unexpended Appropriations		85,502
Change In Net Position		439,030
Net Position - Beginning of Year, as Restated (Note 16)		2,706,446
Net Position - End of Year	$	**3,145,476**

The accompanying notes are an integral part of these financial statements.

U.S. Fish and Wildlife Service
COMBINED STATEMENT OF BUDGETARY RESOURCES
For the year ended September 30, 2001
(dollars in thousands)

Budgetary Resources

Budget Authority	$	2,115,247
Unobligated Balances Beginning of Year (Note 17)		464,209
Spending Authority From Offsetting Collections		120,164
Other Adjustments (Note 17)		96,348
Total Budgetary Resources	$	2,795,968

Status of Budgetary Resources

Obligations Incurred	$	2,096,909
Unobligated Balance, Available		669,875
Unobligated Balance, Not Available		29,184
Total Status of Budgetary Resources	$	2,795,968

Relationship of Obligations to Outlays

Total Obligations Incurred	$	2,096,909
Spending Authority From Offsetting Collections and Adjustments		(219,376)
Obligated Balance, Net - Beginning of Year		864,071
Obligated Balance, Net - End of Year		(1,015,233)
Total Outlays	$	1,726,371

The accompanying notes are an integral part of these financial statements.

U.S. Fish and Wildlife Service
CONSOLIDATED STATEMENT OF FINANCING
For the year ended September 30, 2001
(dollars in thousands)

Obligations and Nonbudgetary Resources

Obligations Incurred	$ 2,096,909
Spending Authority from Offsetting Collections and Adjustments	(219,376)
Donations Not in the Budget	(291)
Financing Imputed for Cost Subsidies	33,084
Transfers, Net	(52,862)
Exchange Revenue Not in the Budget	(648)
Appropriated Revenue	(33,999)
Total Obligations, as Adjusted, and Nonbudgetary Resources	$ **1,822,817**

Less: Resources That Do Not Fund Net Cost of Operations

Change in Amount of Goods, Services, and Benefits Ordered but Not Yet Received or Provided	163,700
Costs Capitalized on the Balance Sheet	84,495
Financing Sources for Unfunded Costs	(9,362)
Other and Prior Period Adjustments	(933)
Total Resources That Do Not Fund Net Cost of Operations	$ **237,900**

Costs That Do Not Require Resources

Depreciation and Amortization	53,311
Bad Debt Expense	188
Loss on Disposition of Assets	6,424
Other	1,351
Total Costs That Do Not Require Resources	$ **61,274**

Financing Sources Yet to Be Provided	(7)
Net Cost of Operations	$ **1,646,184**

The accompanying notes are an integral part of these financial statements.

Notes to
Principal Financial Statements
as of September 30, 2001 and 2000

Note 1. Summary of Significant Accounting Principles

A. Reporting Entity

The United States Fish and Wildlife Service (Service) is a Bureau within the Department of the Interior (Department), which is a cabinet-level agency of the Executive Branch of the Federal Government. The Service is responsible for conserving, protecting, and enhancing fish, wildlife and plants and their habitats for the continuing benefit of the American people. Authority over money, or other budget authority made available to the Service, is vested in the Service's Director, who is responsible for administrative oversight and policy direction of the Service. Accounts are maintained which restrict the use of money (or other budget authority) for use consistent with the purposes and the time period authorized. These accounts also provide assurance that obligations do not exceed authorized amounts.

B. Basis of Accounting and Presentation

The accompanying financial statements reflect both accrual and budgetary accounting transactions. Under the accrual method, revenues are recognized when earned and expenses are recognized when a liability is incurred, without regard to receipt or payment of cash. Budgetary accounting principles, by contrast, are designed to recognize the obligation of funds according to legal requirements, which may be prior to the occurrence of an accrual-based transaction. The recognition of budgetary accounting transactions facilitates compliance with legal constraints and controls over the use of Federal funds. The accompanying financial statements report the financial position, net cost of operations, changes in net position, budgetary resources, and financing of the Service as required by the Chief Financial Officers Act of 1990, as amended by the Reports Consolidation Act of 2000, and the Government Management Reform Act of 1994. The financial statements have been prepared from the books and records of the Service except for certain amounts relating to the Aquatic Resources Trust Fund (ARTF), which were provided by the Department of the Treasury. The financial statements are in conformance with accounting principles generally accepted in the United States of America using guidance issued by the Federal Accounting Standards Advisory Board, instructions specified by the Office of Management and Budget (OMB) on the form and content for entity financial statements, and the policies of the Service and the Department. The Service maintains accounts in four separate fund types and in one clearing account:

1. *General Funds* – These funds are expenditure accounts used to record financial transactions arising from Congressional appropriations or other authorizations to spend general revenues. The principal general funds are:
   a. Resource Management
   b. Construction
   c. Cooperative Endangered Species Conservation
   d. National Wildlife Refuge Fund
   e. North American Wetlands Conservation Fund
   f. Wildlife Conservation and Appreciation Fund
   g. Multi-National Species Fund
   h. Commercial Salmon Program

2. *Trust Funds* – These funds were established to carry out specific programs under trust agreements and statutes. The Service maintains two trust fund accounts:
   a. The Sport Fish Restoration Account (SFRA) makes grants available to States for support projects that restore, conserve, manage, protect, and enhance sport fish resources and coastal wetlands, and also for projects that provide for public use and benefits from sport fish resources. The source of funding for the SFRA is the ARTF, which receives revenues through excise taxes levied on the sale of fishing tackle and equipment, certain motorboat and small engine gasoline, and interest earned on

invested trust funds. The bulk of the excise tax revenues are from gasoline sales, which are deposited into the Highway Trust Fund administered by the Department of Transportation. Gasoline excise tax revenues are subsequently made available to the ARTF by the Department of the Treasury. In addition to the SFRA, the ARTF funds boating safety programs conducted by the U.S. Coast Guard, and also coastal wetlands initiatives conducted by the Corps of Engineers. Title 26 of the U.S. Code, Section 9602 designates the Department of the Treasury as manager of the ARTF, with overall responsibility for the fund's accounting and investment activities. Although the Secretary of the Treasury is responsible by statute for the balances in the ARTF, it is presented on the Service's financial statements in accordance with the requirements of Statement of Federal Financial Accounting Concepts (SFFAC) Number 2, Entity and Display. SFFAC Number 2 requires trust funds that finance multiple programs to be reported by the entity with the preponderance of fund activity. This is also consistent with OMB guidance for financial reporting, which cites Statement of Federal Financial Accounting Standards Number 7, Paragraph 87, as applying to the ARTF. In FY 2001, the SFRA received approximately 79% of the ARTF transfers. ARTF amounts presented on the accompanying financial statements relating to funds not made available to the SFRA and other programs as of September 30, 2001, were provided by the Department of the Treasury. In prior years the ARTF was presented in the Department of Transportation's financial statements. Note 15 provides additional detail on the ARTF.

  b. The Contributed Fund receives contributions from the public for initiatives relating to endangered species recovery, refuge operation and maintenance, research, and other projects in support of the Service's mission.

3. Receipt Funds – These funds arise from the sovereign and regulatory powers unique to the Federal Government. Receipts primarily include miscellaneous fines and penalties, administrative fees, and interest.

4. Special Funds – These funds are receipt accounts that are earmarked by law for a specific purpose, but are not generated from a continuing cycle of operations. Most of these receipts are available immediately. Special fund expenditure accounts record amounts appropriated from special fund receipts, which are used for special programs, as specified by law. The principal special funds are:
  a. Land Acquisition (subject to appropriation)
  b. Federal Aid/Wildlife Restoration
  c. Federal Aid/Sport Fish Restoration
  d. Operation/Maintenance – Quarters
  e. Proceeds from Sales – Water Resources Development Projects
  f. Migratory Bird Conservation
  g. North American Wetlands Conservation
  h. National Wildlife Refuge
  i. Cooperative Endangered Species Conservation (subject to appropriation)
  j. Recreational Fee Demonstration Program
  k. Lahontan Valley and Pyramid Lake Fish and Wildlife Fund

5. Clearing Accounts – These accounts consist of unclassified transactions where there is a reasonable presumption that the amounts belong to the Federal Government.

C. Fund Balance with Treasury
The Service maintains all cash accounts with Treasury except for imprest fund accounts. The funds with Treasury include appropriated, special receipts, and trust funds, which are available to pay current liabilities and outstanding obligations. Cash receipts and disbursements of the Service are processed by Treasury, and the Service's accounts are reconciled with those of Treasury on a regular basis.

D. Investments in Treasury Securities
The Service invests funds from the Federal Aid Wildlife Restoration Fund (Treasury Symbol 14X5029) in Federal Government securities that include marketable Treasury securities and non-marketable par value or non-marketable market-based securities issued by the Federal Investment Branch of the Bureau of Public Debt. Par value securities are special issue bonds or certificates of indebtedness that bear interest determined by legislation or the Treasury. Market-based securities are Treasury

securities that are not traded on any securities exchange, but mirror the prices of marketable securities with similar terms. The Service intends to hold these investments until maturity. Investments are valued at cost and adjusted for amortization of premiums and discounts, if applicable. The premiums and discounts are recognized as adjustments to interest income, utilizing the straight-line method. No provision is made for unrealized gains or losses on these securities. Interest on investments is accrued as it is earned.

The Service also reports investments of the ARTF (Treasury Symbol 20X8147) managed by Treasury (see Note 1.B.2.). Although the Service has advisory authority for ARTF investment decisions, the Treasury has legal responsibility for investing ARTF funds. Consistent with authorizing legislation and Treasury fiscal investment policies, the Secretary of the Treasury invests such portion of the ARTF balance deemed by the program agencies not necessary to meet current withdrawals to cover program and related costs as defined by law. Such investments are in non-marketable par value or non-marketable market-based securities as authorized by legislation and are issued and redeemed by the Federal Investment Branch of the Bureau of Public Debt, in the Department of Treasury. These securities are held in the name of the Secretary of Treasury for the ARTF and interest in investments is accrued as it is earned. The premiums and discounts are recognized as adjustments to interest income, utilizing the effective interest method. Although funds collected and deposited in the ARTF in any one fiscal year are available for investment during the same fiscal year collected, they are not available for obligation that same year. Thus, the use of such funds collected from a prior fiscal year is restricted until the following fiscal year. Note 5 provides additional information on Service and ARTF investments.

E. Accounts Receivable
Receivables represent amounts owed to the Service by other Federal agencies and the public, (with the exception of amounts owed to the ARTF and reported by the Service), and include accounts receivable, interest receivable and taxes receivable. Accounts receivable primarily arise from the provision of goods and services or from the levy of fines and penalties resulting from the Service's regulatory responsibilities. Taxes receivable consist entirely of tax receipts owed to the ARTF, which serves as the funding source for the Sport Fish Restoration Account, one of two trust funds maintained by the Service. Interest receivable consists primarily of amounts earned but not yet received from Service investments and ARTF investments reported by the Service. An allowance for doubtful accounts is maintained to reflect uncollectible receivables from the public. The allowance amount is estimated based on an average of prior year write-offs and an analysis of outstanding accounts receivable. Federal accounts receivable are considered to be fully collectible. Note 6 provides additional information concerning receivables.

F. Operating Materials and Supplies
Operating materials and supplies consist of items such as lumber, sand, gravel, and other items purchased in large quantities which will be consumed in future operations. Operating materials and supplies are accounted for based on the purchase method. Under this method, operating materials and supplies are expensed when purchased.

G. General Property, Plant and Equipment (PP&E)
General property, plant and equipment consist of buildings, structures, facilities and equipment used in the operation of wildlife refuges, fish hatcheries, wildlife and fishery research centers, waterfowl production areas, and administrative sites. Capitalized buildings and structures have a cumulative acquisition cost of $50,000 or more. Buildings are comprised of facilities owned by the Service, such as houses, garages, shops, schools, laboratories, and other buildings. Structures and facilities owned by the Service include powerhouses and pumping plants, structural and general service facilities systems (e.g., drainage, plumbing, sewer, ventilating, water or heating systems), ground and site improvements (e.g., roads and roadways, fences, lawns, shrubbery, parking areas, sidewalks, sprinkler systems, yard drainage systems, or yard lighting systems), bridges and trestles, dams and dikes, waterways and wells. Capitalized costs include materials, labor, and overhead costs incurred during construction, attorney and architect fees, and building permits. Depreciation is recorded using the straight-line method based on an estimated useful life of 10 to 30 years.

Buildings and property are reported in the financial statements based on legal ownership.

The Service also leases PP&E for its operations. All of the Service's leases are considered operating leases in which the Service does not assume the risks of ownership of the PP&E. Note 12 provides additional information on the Service's operating leases.

Consistent with accounting standards for PP&E, most land managed by the Service is reported as stewardship land in the Supplementary Stewardship Information section of the annual report. Land associated with administrative sites is reported on the accompanying financial statements.

Capitalized equipment consists of those assets, other than buildings or other structures, which have an estimated useful life of greater than one year and an initial acquisition cost exceeding $25,000. Depreciation is recorded using the straight-line method based on the estimated useful life of the respective assets of five to ten years. Note 7 provides additional information on the Service's PP&E.

H. Seized and Forfeited Property
Property seized by or forfeited to the Service consists primarily of wildlife and wildlife products. A smaller number of non-wildlife property items, such as guns, ammunition or forensic evidence, is also seized by or forfeited to the Service. The Service is responsible for safeguarding seized and forfeited property from the time of seizure through the final disposition of the property. Methods of disposing seized and forfeited property include retaining the property in the Service for educational purposes, transferring the property to other Federal entities, returning the property to the owner, or disposing of the property through destruction, sale, donation or other methods authorized by law. Property for which a legal market exists is reported at appraised value or at values received at auction. Property that cannot be sold (e.g., all or parts of migratory birds, bald and golden eagles, endangered or threatened species, marine mammals, and species listed on Appendix I to the Convention on International Trade in Endangered Species) is classified as "non-marketable" and has no legal value. Note 8 provides additional information on seized property. There was no forfeited property reported as of September 30, 2001.

I. Liabilities and Contingencies
A liability for Federal accounting purposes is a probable and measurable outflow or other sacrifice of resources as a result of past transactions or events. Intragovernmental liabilities arise from transactions with other Federal agencies. Liabilities Not Covered by Budgetary Resources result from the receipt of goods or services, or the occurrence of events, for which budgetary resources are not available. A liability cannot be paid absent appropriation of funds by Congress, and there is no certainty that such budgetary resources will be provided. The Federal Government, acting in its sovereign capacity, can abrogate those liabilities that arise for reasons other than through contracts.

Unearned revenue is recorded as deferred revenue until earned. The majority of deferred revenue represents obligated balances for funds made available through Title V (Priority Land Acquisitions, Land Exchanges, and Maintenance) of Public Law 105-83, dated November 14, 1997 (111 Stat. 1610), and pursuant to Title VI of the Department of Interior and Related Agencies Appropriations Act (PL. 106-113), 2000.

The Federal Employees' Compensation Act (FECA) liability is the liability for future workers' compensation. This includes the expected liability for death, disability, medical, and miscellaneous costs for approved cases. The liability is determined using a method that utilizes historical benefit payment patterns related to a specific incurred period to predict the utlitmate payments related to that period.

Liabilities of the ARTF are the amounts of funds resulting from the original budget authority for a fiscal year less the cash drawdowns transferred during that same fiscal year.

Contingent liabilities relate to conditions, situations, or circumstances where the existence or amount of the liability cannot be determined with certainty pending the outcome of future events. The Service recognizes contingent liabilities when a future outflow or other sacrifice of resources is measurable and probable.

J. Revenues and Other Financing Sources
The Service receives the majority of the funding needed to support its programs through appropriations. The Service receives annual, multi-year, and no-year appropriations that may be used within statutory limits for operating expenses and capital expenditures. Additional amounts are obtained through reimbursements for services provided to public entities and other Federal agencies in accordance with reimbursable agreements. Receipts from reimbursable agreements are recognized as revenues when earned, and may be used to offset the cost of operations, including indirect costs.

Significant funding is made available to support Service programs from tax revenues, which are recognized when earned. These tax revenues emanate from excise taxes, collected from manufacturers of equipment used in hunting, fishing, sport shooting on ranges, and on motorboat fuels, which are deposited into either the Wildlife Restoration Fund or the ARTF.

K. Annual, Sick and Other Leave
Annual leave is accrued as it is earned. The accrual is reduced as leave is taken. Each year, the balance in the accrued annual leave account is adjusted to reflect current pay rates. To the extent current or prior year appropriations are not available to fund annual leave, future funding sources will be used.

Sick leave and other types of non-vested leave are expensed as taken. Accrued benefits are included in Intragovernmental Liabilities.

L. Retirement Plans
Service employees participate in either the Civil Service Retirement System (CSRS) or the Federal Employees Retirement System (FERS) defined-benefit pension plans. FERS went into effect January 1, 1987. FERS and Social Security automatically cover most employees hired after December 31, 1983. FERS offers a savings plan to which the Service automatically contributes one percent of basic pay and matches employee contributions up to four percent of basic pay. Employees hired prior to January 1, 1984 could elect to either join FERS and Social Security, or remain in CSRS. The Service contributes an amount equal to one percent of the employee's basic pay to the tax deferred Thrift Savings Plan and matches employee contributions up to an additional four percent of basic pay. As of September 30, 2001, FERS employees could contribute up to 11 percent of their gross earnings to the plan. CSRS employees were limited to a contribution of six percent of their gross earnings to the plan and receive no matching contribution from the Service.

The Service is not responsible for and does not report CSRS or FERS assets, accumulated plan benefits, or liabilities applicable to its employees. The Office of Personnel Management (OPM), which administers the plans, is responsible for and reports these amounts.

M. Statement of Net Cost of Operations (SNC)
The format of the FY 2000 SNC has been revised to present the organizational structure that is primarily responsible for carrying out Service mission and goals. The organization breakout is consistent with the Service's budget and performance plans. The FY 2000 SNC is unaudited.

N. Comparative Data
The Balance Sheet and SNC present comparative data for the prior fiscal year, in order to provide an understanding of changes in the Service's financial position and its net cost. Portions of the FY 2000 data have been restated to be comparative. Note 16 provides additional information on the restatements.

Note 2. Entity and Non-Entity Assets

The assets reported in the financial statements include unrestricted entity assets, restricted entity assets, and non-entity assets. Unrestricted entity assets are currently available for use by the Service. Restricted entity assets are not currently available for use by the Service, pending transfer of funds from the ARTF to the SFRA. A portion of the ARTF assets are transferred to the U.S. Coast Guard and the Corps of Engineers and are reflected as non-entity assets. Non-entity assets are held by the Service with no authority to spend, and will be forwarded to other agencies at a future date. The following chart summarizes the Service's non-entity, restricted entity, and unrestricted entity assets as of September 30, 2001 and 2000 (dollars in thousands):

	2001	2000
Intragovernmental:		
Fund Balance with Treasury	$ 6,600	$ 6,888
Investments, Net	335,416	299,258
Total Non-Entity Assets	342,016	306,146
Entity Assets:		
Restricted	982,607	923,892
Unrestricted	2,468,732	2,091,620
Total Entity Assets	3,451,339	3,015,512
Total Assets	$ 3,793,355	$ 3,321,658

Note 3. Fund Balance with Treasury

The fund balance with Treasury as of September 30, 2001 and 2000 is as follows (dollars in thousands):

	2001	2000
Fund Balance:		
Operating Funds	$546,825	$470,074
Trust Funds	36,162	21,554
Unavailable Receipt Funds	149,195	176,400
Special Receipt Funds	462,160	239,469
Total Fund Balance with Treasury	$1,194,342	$907,497

	2001	2000
Status of Fund Balance with Treasury		
Unobligated Balance		
Available	$655,833	$410,958
Unavailable	3,725	3,188
Obligated Balance Not Yet Disbursed	842,394	713,280
Available, Restricted Use		
Imprest Funds, Investments, and Discounts on Investments	(476,021)	(406,378)
Fund Balance Not Supported by Appropriated Funds		
Suspense Accounts, Unavailable Receipt Accounts and		
Aquatic Resources Trust Fund	168,411	186,449
Total Fund Balance with Treasury	$1,194,342	$907,497

Note 4. Cash

Cash consists of petty cash imprest funds of approximately $140,000 and $458,000 as of September 30, 2001 and 2000, respectively.

Note 5. Investments

Investments in non-marketable market-based Treasury securities consist of various bills purchased through the Federal Investment Branch of the Bureau of Public Debt. The invested funds consist of excise tax receipts from the Federal Aid in Wildlife Restoration Fund (Treasury Symbol 14X5029), and the ARTF (Treasury Symbol 20X8147). Outstanding investments in Treasury securities as of September 30, 2001 and 2000 total (dollars in thousands):

	2001	2000
14X5029		
Acquisition Cost	$479,068	$406,632
Unamortized Premium/(Discount)	(737)	(395)
Net Investments	478,331	406,237
Market Value	478,787	406,338
ARTF (20X8147)		
Acquisition Cost	1,304,233	1,191,880
Unamortized Premium/(Discount)	(10,508)	(442)
Net Investments	1,293,725	1,191,438
Market Value	1,295,118	1,189,502
Total Net Investments	1,772,056	1,597,675
Total Market Value	$1,773,905	$1,595,840

Note 6. Receivables

Accounts and interest receivable consist of amounts owed the Service by other Federal agencies and the public and are recognized primarily when the Service performs reimbursable services or sells goods. Accounts receivable also includes those funds, including taxes receivable, deposited in the ARTF. Interest receivable consists of monies earned but not yet received and these monies primarily derive from investments disclosed in Note 5. Accounts and interest receivable as of September 30, 2001 and 2000 consist of (dollars in thousands):

	2001		2000	
	Intragovernmental	With the Public	Intragovernmental	With the Public
Accounts Receivable				
Accounts Receivable, Gross	$22,344	$7,898	$25,084	$5,328
Allowance	-	(456)	-	(340)
Accounts Receivable, Net	22,344	7,442	25,084	4,988
Taxes Receivable				
Taxes Receivable, Gross	6,352	-	22,833	-
Allowance	-	-	-	-
Taxes Receivable, Net	6,352	-	22,833	-
Total Accounts and Taxes Receivable, Net	28,696	7,442	47,917	4,988
Interest Receivable				
Interest Receivable, Gross	4,791	71	3,270	47
Allowance	-	(16)	-	-
Interest Receivable, Net	$4,791	$55	$3,270	$47

Note 7. Property, Plant and Equipment (PP&E)

General PP&E owned by the Service as of September 30, 2001 and 2000 consists of the following (dollars in thousands):

	Acquisition Value		Accumulated Depreciation		Net Book Value	
	2001	2000	2001	2000	2001	2000
Land	$ 10,538	$ 10,508	$ -	$ -	$ 10,538	$ 10,508
Buildings	459,427	448,253	167,745	150,445	291,682	297,808
Other Structures	566,846	537,688	265,112	250,103	301,734	287,585
Subtotal Buildings and Structures	1,026,273	985,941	432,857	400,548	593,416	585,393
Construction in Progress	85,390	82,829	-	-	85,390	82,829
Equipment	216,469	189,979	122,698	110,354	93,771	79,625
Total	$1,338,670	$1,269,257	$ 555,555	$ 510,902	$ 783,115	$ 758,355

Note 8. Seized and Forfeited Property

Seized and forfeited property is recorded in case files maintained in the Service's Law Enforcement Management Information System (LEMIS 2000). The Service does not assign a financial value to, or recognize for purposes of its financial statements, property seized by or forfeited to the Service that cannot be sold due to legal restrictions. Such property is typically wildlife or wildlife parts and can be donated to schools, aquaria, museums, or zoos for educational or scientific purposes. Seized or forfeited property that can be sold legally is valued by individual agents based on their best professional estimate, through declarations, or through evaluating fair market value. These marketable property values are entered into the case file in LEMIS 2000 and are reported below.

There was no forfeited property reported as of September 30, 2001. Based on an evaluation of Law Enforcement property values, there is no seized property in the financial statements. Seized property cases and values as of September 30, 2001 and 2000, are displayed below (dollars in thousands):

	2001		2000	
	# of Cases	Market Value	# of Cases	Market Value
Seized Property	1,747	$1,937	599	$2,235
Property Dispositions	2,282	4,475	2,288	4,605

Note 9. Liabilities Not Covered by Budgetary Resources

These liabilities are claims against the Service by other Federal and non-Federal entities. Liabilities not covered by budgetary resources as of September 30, 2001 and 2000 are as follows (dollars in thousands):

	2001		2000	
	Intragovernmental	With the Public	Intragovernmental	With the Public
Unfunded Annual Leave	$0	$37,153	$0	$35,827
Actuarial FECA Liability	0	52,882	0	51,949
Unfunded FECA Liability	10,151	0	9,069	0
Environmental Cleanup Liabilities	0	46,807	0	42,000
Total Other Liabilities Not Covered by Budgetary Resources	$10,151	$136,842	$9,069	$129,776

Note 10. Environmental Cleanup Liabilities

The Service operates its environmental cleanup program in accordance with the requirements of the Resource Conservation and Recovery Act and the Comprehensive Environmental Response, Compensation, and Liability Act and cleanup regulations established by the Environmental Protection Agency. Environmental liabilities for the Service are associated with the future costs of remediating hazardous waste and landfills existing within units of the National Wildlife Refuge System (NWRS) and the National Fish Hatcheries System (NFHS). The Service believes that a reasonable estimate of the future costs of cleaning certain contamination within the NWRS and the NFHS is approximately $46.8 million as of September 30, 2001. (The Service estimated its environmental cleanup liabilities as of September 30, 2000 to be approximately $42 million.) The change in the liability estimates between FY 2000 and FY 2001 results from changes in the estimates for total cleanup costs. This estimate of future costs includes sites on lands obtained by the Service through donation, acquisition or transfer from other agencies. Cost estimates are based on preliminary investigations of known sites and the expected degree and type of contamination probable at these sites. It does not include sites unknown, sites for which Service responsibility is unclear, sites that have not been investigated, or sites degraded by offsite activities beyond the control of the Service. Where possible, cost estimates are included for conducting site investigations and for conducting monitoring actions needed to assess the efficacy of cleanup. The Service's methods for estimating these liabilities include quotes from private firms or government agencies that have worked on the sites, projected planning figures based on related projects, and best engineering judgment.

Note 11. Contingent Liabilities

In FY 2001, the Service is involved with one lawsuit with a potential liability estimated at $1 million. The Service has a defense in this case and expects to prevail in court or otherwise settle the case for an amount substantially less than the amount sought by the plaintiffs. In the opinion of the Service management, as well as the Office of the Solicitor, resolution of this case will not materially affect the financial position, results of operations, or cash flows of the Service. Any amounts paid by the Government will be paid out of the Judgment Fund of the U.S. Department of the Treasury rather than Service appropriations. No amounts have been accrued in the financial records because the amount of award cannot be accurately predicted at this time.

Note 12. Operating Leases

Real Property: Most of the Service's facilities are rented from the General Services Administration (GSA), which charges rent that is intended to approximate commercial rental rates. The Service includes the estimated rental payments to GSA in the table that follows. For Federally-owned facilities, the Service generally does not execute an agreement with GSA; however, the Service is normally required to give 120 to 180 days notice if it intends to vacate. For non-Federally owned property an occupancy agreement is generally executed, according to standard contract principles.

The estimates for personal property represent the cost of leasing GSA vehicles. The Service's estimates in the near-term are based on an annual inflation factor of 3 percent, which is approximately $58,000 per year through FY 2004. Estimates for FY 2005 and FY 2006 are based on a 4.4 percent increase from the latest GSA cost per square foot annual increase. The aggregate estimates for the Service's: (1) future payments due under non-Federal or noncancellable operating leases; and (2) estimated real property rent payments to GSA and other Federal entities as of September 30, 2001, are as follows (dollars in thousands):

Fiscal Year	PP&E Category		Total
	Real Property	Personal Property	
2002	$41,623	$1,723	$43,346
2003	44,326	1,775	46,101
2004	45,256	1,828	47,084
2005	47,247	1,883	49,130
2006	49,326	1,939	51,265
Total Future Lease Payments	$227,778	$9,148	$236,926

Note 13. Net Position

Net position consists of unexpended appropriations and cumulative results of operations. Unexpended appropriations represent amounts of budget authority that include unobligated balances and obligated balances that are not rescinded or withheld. Obligations represent amounts designated for payment for goods and services ordered but not received (undelivered orders). Unexpended appropriations include only those appropriations associated with resources received from Treasury's General Fund. Appropriations realized and recorded as budget authority from special receipt revenues that do not flow through Treasury's General Fund are considered part of cumulative results of operations. Unexpended Appropriations as of September 30, 2001 and 2000 are as follows (dollars in thousands):

	2001	2000
Unexpended Appropriations		
Unobligated - Available	$142,436	$130,208
Unavailable	19,732	2,822
Undelivered Orders	303,879	247,515
Total Unexpended Appropriations	$466,047	$380,545

Note 14. Imputed Financing Sources

Imputed financing sources are amounts equal to the costs that have been incurred by the reporting entity and budgeted by another entity when services are received at less than full cost. The Service recognizes the actuarial present value of pensions and other retirement benefits for its employees during their active years of service. By recognizing non-budgetary resources, as with the imputed cost of approximately $33 million, the Service's accompanying financial statements reflect the recorded costs that were financed by budgetary resources of the OPM.

Note 15. Aquatic Resources Trust Fund (ARTF)

The Service's financial statements reflect balances of the ARTF (20X8147) which provides funding sources to the SFRA and balances which are distributed to the U.S. Coast Guard Boat Safety Program and the Army Corps of Engineers Coastal Wetlands Program. The table below reflects summarized information of the ARTF as of September 30, 2001 and 2000 (dollars in thousands).

	Aquatic Resources Trust Fund	
	2001	2000
Fund Balance with Treasury	$17,671	$8,540
Investments, Net	1,293,724	1,191,438
Taxes Receivable, Net	6,352	22,833
Interest Receivable, Net	276	339
Total Assets	1,318,023	1,223,150
Invested Balances:		
Fish and Wildlife Service	410,832	405,062
Payable to:		
Corps of Engineers	265,321	235,661
Coast Guard	70,095	63,596
Subtotal for Payables	335,416	299,258
Total Invested Balances	746,248	704,319
Total Net Position	571,775	518,831
Total Liabilities and Net Position	$1,318,023	$1,223,150
Tax and Interest Revenue	470,874	439,511
Net Transfers	(417,930)	(384,378)
Total Changes in Fund Balance	52,944	55,133
Net Position, Beginning of Year	518,831	463,697
Net Position, End of Year	$571,775	$518,831

Note 16. Restatements and Reclassifications

Restatements and reclassifications are used to reflect the retroactive impact of changes to accounting or reporting policies and correction of errors in the prior period. The Service restated its beginning FY 2000 financial statements to reflect the change in reporting policy and correct errors from prior periods as follows:

- $518,831 to record balances of the Aquatic Resources Trust Fund including Fund Balance with Treasury, Investments, Invested Balances, and Net Position.
- $18,553 to remove buildings and related accumulated depreciation as a result of errors in depreciation and to remove assets that should have been removed in prior years.
- $19,240 to record accounts payable for unbilled grantee expense.

The FY 2000 balances have been restated as follows (dollars in thousands):

	2000 As Previously Reported	Restatements	2000 As Restated
Fund Balance with Treasury	$898,957	$8,540	$907,497
Investments - Treasury Securities	406,237	1,191,438	1,597,675
Accounts and Taxes Receivable, Net	430,145	(382,228)	47,917
Interest Receivable	2,978	339	3,317
Property, Plant, and Equipment	776,908	(18,553)	758,355
Accounts Payable with the Public	50,905	19,240	70,145
Payable for Invested Balances	-	299,258	299,258
Unexpended Appropriations	380,575	(30)	380,545
Cumulative Results of Operations	1,844,833	481,068	2,325,901
Net Position	$2,225,408	$481,038	$2,706,446

In addition, certain prior year amounts have been reclassified to conform to the current year presentation.

Note 17. Statement of Budgetary Resources Adjustments

Budgetary resources do not include $198,486,000 in appropriations available for investment, but not available for obligation at September, 30, 2001. Differences between the Statement of Budgetary Resources and the Report on Budget Execution - SF 133 are as follows (dollars in thousands):

Prior Year Unobligated Balance, Net	$25,000
Budget Authority Not Reported in FACTS II (1469X8083)	
Federal Aid Highways	12,163
Total Differences	**$37,163**
Other Adjustments	
Rescissions	($2,864)
Downward Adjustments	99,212
Total Other Adjustments	**$96,348**
Other	
Budgetary Resources Available for Investment Not Obligation Not Included On the Statement of Budgetary Resources	$198,486

Note 18. Net Cost

The following schedule fully displays net cost of operations by classifying detailed revenue and cost information by responsibility segment, which supports the summary information in the SNC.

Consolidating Statement of Net Cost
Year Ended September 30, 2001 and 2000
(dollars in thousands)

	Endangered Species	Fisheries and Habitat Conservation	Law Enforcement	Migratory Birds & State Programs	National Wildlife Refuge System	International Affairs	General Operations	Elimination of Intra-Bureau Activity	2001	(Unaudited) 2000
Sustainability of Fish and Wildlife Populations										
Gross Cost	$133,915	$85,039	$50,819	$148,343	$49,675	$10,255	$120,033	-	$598,079	$596,681
Earned Revenue	3,232	35,385	6,161	289	2,280	197	1,827	-	49,371	40,903
Net Cost	$130,683	$49,654	$44,658	$148,054	$47,395	$10,058	$118,206	$0	$548,708	$555,778
Habitat Conservation: A Network of Land and Water										
Gross Cost	41,766	127,210	-	392,351	239,788	-	227,703	-	1,028,818	933,941
Earned Revenue	-	30,092	3	25,796	24,072	-	4,961	-	84,924	82,589
Net Cost	$41,766	$97,118	($3)	$366,555	$215,716	$0	$222,742	$0	$943,894	$851,352
Public Use and Enjoyment										
Gross Cost		17,771	-	22,605	91,586	-	29,486	-	161,448	180,321
Earned Revenue	-	6,437	-	139	4,076	-	626	-	11,278	11,898
Net Cost	$0	$11,334	$0	$22,466	$87,510	$0	$28,860	$0	$150,170	$168,423
Partnerships in Natural Resources										
Gross Cost	-	-	-	-	-	-	3,445	-	3,445	-
Earned Revenue	-	-	-	-	-	-	33	-	33	-
Net Cost	$0	$0	$0	$0	$0	$0	$3,412	-	$3,412	$0
Eliminations and Other										
Gross Cost	-	-	-	-	-	-	-	(584)	(584)	(519)
Earned Revenue	-	-	-	-	-	-	-	(584)	(584)	(625)
Net Cost	$0	$0	$0	$0	$0	$0	$0	$0	$0	$106
Totals										
Gross Cost	175,681	230,020	50,819	563,299	381,049	10,255	380,667	(584)	1,791,206	1,710,424
Earned Revenue	3,232	71,914	6,164	26,224	30,428	197	7,447	(584)	145,022	134,765
Net Cost of Operations	$172,449	$158,106	$44,655	$537,075	$350,621	$10,058	$373,220	$0	$1,646,184	$1,575,659

Required Supplementary Information

The following statement provides greater detail on the sources of funding as presented in the *Combined Statement of Budgetary Resources.*

U.S. Fish and Wildlife Service
Required Supplementary Information
COMBINING STATEMENT OF BUDGETARY RESOURCES
For the year ended September 30, 2001
(dollars in thousands)

	Operating Funds	Special Receipt Funds	Trust Funds	Total
Budgetary Resources				
Budget Authority	$ 1,073,316	$ 727,457	$ 314,474	$ 2,115,247
Unobligated Balances Beginning of Year	190,357	161,003	112,849	464,209
Spending Authority From Offsetting Collections	111,143	9,021	-	120,164
Other Adjustments	18,756	33,586	44,006	96,348
Total Budgetary Resources	$ 1,393,572	$ 931,067	$ 471,329	$ 2,795,968
Status of Budgetary Resources				
Obligations Incurred	$ 1,186,757	$ 565,654	$ 344,498	$ 2,096,909
Unobligated Balance, Available	177,637	365,407	126,831	669,875
Unobligated Balance, Not Available	29,178	6	-	29,184
Total Status of Budgetary Resources	$ 1,393,572	$ 931,067	$ 471,329	$ 2,795,968
Relationship of Obligations to Outlays				
Total Obligations Incurred	$ 1,186,757	$ 565,654	$ 344,498	$ 2,096,909
Spending Authority From Offsetting Collections and Adjustments	(132,013)	(43,357)	(44,006)	(219,376)
Obligated Balance, Net - Beginning of Year	278,725	280,120	305,226	864,071
Obligated Balance, Net - End of Year	(338,457)	(374,283)	(302,493)	(1,015,233)
Total Outlays	$ 995,012	$ 428,134	$ 303,225	$ 1,726,371

See accompanying independent auditors' report.

United States Department of the Interior

Office of Inspector General
Washington, D.C. 20240

MAR 2 5 2002

Memorandum

To: Director, U.S. Fish and Wildlife Service

From: Roger La Rouche
         Assistant Inspector General for Audits

Subject: Independent Auditors' Report on the U.S. Fish and Wildlife Service's Financial
         Statements for Fiscal Years 2001 and 2000 (No. 2002-I-0025)

We contracted with KPMG, LLP, an independent certified public accounting
firm, to audit the U.S. Fish and Wildlife Service's (FWS) financial statements for fiscal
year 2001. The contract required that KPMG conduct its audit in accordance with the
Government Auditing Standards issued by the Comptroller General of the United States
of America; Office of Management and Budget Bulletin 01-02, *Audit Requirements for
Federal Financial Statements*; and the General Accounting Office/President's Council on
Integrity and Efficiency *Financial Audit Manual*. The Office of Inspector General (OIG)
is responsible for the opinion on the consolidated balance sheet and related notes for
fiscal year 2000.

In connection with the contract, we monitored the progress of the audit at key
points and reviewed KPMG's report and related working papers and inquired of their
representatives. Our review, as differentiated from an audit in accordance with
Government Auditing Standards, was not intended to enable us to express, and we do not
express, opinions on the FWS's financial statements or on conclusions about the
effectiveness of internal controls or on conclusions about compliance with laws and
regulations. KPMG is responsible for the auditors' report on the fiscal year 2001
financial statements (Attachment 1) and for the conclusions expressed in the report.
However, our review disclosed no instances where KPMG did not comply in all material
respects with *Government Auditing Standards*.

In its audit report dated January 21, 2002 KPMG stated that in its opinion the
FWS's financial statements for fiscal year 2001 present fairly, in all material respects, the
financial position of FWS as of September 30, 2001, and its net cost, changes in net
position, budgetary resources, and reconciliation of net cost to budgetary obligations for
the year then ended, in conformity with accounting principles generally accepted in the
United States of America. In our audit report dated January 21, 2002 (Attachment 2) we
stated that in our opinion the FWS's balance sheet presents fairly, in all material respects,

the financial position of the FWS as of September 30, 2000 in conformity with accounting principles generally accepted in the United States of America.

KPMG found four material weaknesses and one reportable condition related to internal controls over financial reporting. With regard to compliance with laws and regulations, KPMG found FWS to be noncompliant with a portion of the Federal Financial Management Improvement Act. Specifically, KPMG reported that the FWS's financial management systems did not substantially comply with EDP security and general control environment requirements, and that identified material weaknesses affected the FWS's ability to prepare its financial statements and related disclosures in accordance with Federal accounting standards.

In the February 21, 2002 response, and in subsequent discussions, the Director, FWS, concurred with Recommendations A, B, C, E, F, and G. The FWS agreed with the general finding for Recommendation D but disagreed that sufficient risk exists to endanger financial management statements or operations. Based on the response and subsequent discussions, all seven recommendations are considered resolved but not implemented. The seven recommendations will be referred to the Assistant Secretary for Policy, Management and Budget for tracking of implementation.

Section 5(a) of the *Inspector General Act* (5 U.S.C. App. 3) requires the OIG to list this report in its semiannual report to the Congress. The Independent Auditors' Report is intended for the information of the management of FWS, the Office of Management and Budget, and the United States Congress. The report, however, is a matter of public record, and its distribution is not limited.

Attachments (2)

2

707 Seventeenth Stree
Suite 2300
Denver, CO 80202

Independent Auditors' Report

The Director of the United States Fish and Wildlife Service and the Inspector General of the Department of the Interior:

We have audited the accompanying consolidated balance sheet of the United States Fish and Wildlife Service (Service) as of September 30, 2001, and the related consolidated statements of net cost, changes in net position, and financing and the combined statement of budgetary resources for the year then ended (hereinafter referred to as financial statements). The objective of our audit was to express an opinion on the fair presentation of these financial statements. In connection with our audit, we also considered the Service's internal control over financial reporting and tested the Service's compliance with certain provisions of applicable laws and regulations that could have a direct and material effect on its financial statements.

Summary

As stated in our opinion on the financial statements, we concluded that the Service's financial statements as of and for the year ended September 30, 2001 are presented fairly, in all material respects, in conformity with accounting principles generally accepted in the United States of America.

Our consideration of internal control over financial reporting resulted in the following matters being identified as reportable conditions:

A.   Financial reporting process

B.   Controls, processes, and financial reporting relating to capital equipment

C.   Controls, processes, and financial reporting relating to buildings, structures, and construction work in process

D.   Security and general controls over financial management systems

E.   Financial reporting of the Sport Fish Restoration account

We consider reportable conditions A through D, discussed above, to be material weaknesses.

The results of our tests of compliance with certain provisions of laws and regulations, exclusive of the *Federal Financial Management Improvement Act of 1996* (FFMIA), disclosed no instances of noncompliance with laws and regulations that are required to be reported under *Government Auditing Standards*, issued by the Comptroller General of the United States, and Office of Management and Budget (OMB) Bulletin No. 01-02, *Audit Requirements for Federal Financial Statements.* However, our tests of compliance with FFMIA section 803(a) requirements disclosed instances where the Service's financial management systems did not substantially comply with the following:

F.   Federal financial management systems requirements

G.   Federal accounting standards

The following sections discuss our opinion on the Service's financial statements, our consideration of the Service's internal control over financial reporting, our tests of the Service's compliance with certain provisions of applicable laws and regulations, and management's and our responsibilities.

Opinion on the Financial Statements

We have audited the accompanying consolidated balance sheet of the Service as of September 30, 2001, and the related consolidated statements of net cost, changes in net position, and financing and the combined statement of budgetary resources for the year then ended.

In our opinion, the financial statements referred to above present fairly, in all material respects, the financial position of the Service as of September 30, 2001, and its net cost, changes in net position, budgetary resources, and reconciliation of net cost to budgetary obligations for the year then ended in conformity with accounting principles generally accepted in the United States of America.

The information included in the Supplementary Stewardship Information, Supplementary Information on Service Performance, and financial highlights of Service Financial Performance sections are not a required part of the financial statements, but is supplementary information required by the Federal Accounting Standards Advisory Board or Office of Management and Budget Bulletin 97-01, *Form and Content of Agency's Financial Statements*, as amended. We have applied certain limited procedures which consisted principally of inquiries of management regarding the methods of measurement and presentation of this information. However, we did not audit this information, and accordingly, we express no opinion on it.

Our audit was conducted for the purpose of forming an opinion on the financial statements taken as a whole. The information in the Combining Statement of Budgetary Resources is presented for purposes of additional analysis and is not a required part of the financial statements. Such information has been subjected to the auditing procedures applied in the audit of the financial statements and, in our opinion, is fairly stated, in all material respects, in relation to the financial statements taken as a whole.

Internal Control Over Financial Reporting

Our consideration of internal control over financial reporting would not necessarily disclose all matters in the internal control over financial reporting that might be reportable conditions. Under standards issued by the American Institute of Certified Public Accountants, reportable conditions are matters coming to our attention relating to significant deficiencies in the design or operation of the internal control over financial reporting that, in our judgment, could adversely affect the Service's ability to record, process, summarize, and report financial data consistent with the assertions of management in the financial statements.

Material weaknesses are reportable conditions in which the design or operation of one or more of the internal control components does not reduce to a relatively low level the risk that misstatements, in amounts that would be material in relation to the financial statements being audited, may occur and not be detected within a timely period by employees in the normal course of performing their assigned functions.

2

Because of inherent limitations in internal control, misstatements due to error or fraud may nevertheless occur and not be detected.

We noted certain matters, discussed below, involving the internal control over financial reporting and its operation that we consider to be reportable conditions. We believe that the following reportable conditions are material weaknesses:

A. Financial Reporting Process

The Service is a large, complex organization that has numerous programs and offices that participate in financial transaction processing and thereby affect financial reporting. Both programs and field offices are responsible for generating transaction data to the National Business Center and Service Finance Center. The Finance Center is responsible for compiling periodic financial reporting to the Department of Treasury as well as the year-end financial statements.

Each year the Service prepares financial statements that disclose the Service's financial position and results of operations. Office of Management and Budget (OMB) Bulletin 97-01, *Form and Content of Agency's Financial Statements,* as amended, provides guidance on the Service's financial statements format and content. Financial reporting is necessary for timely and accurate information for business decision making.

Financial Reporting and Analysis. The Service's current financial reporting is untimely, manually intensive, and prone to error. Also, many of the Service's current analyses focus on post-transaction review, designed to detect errors, rather than thorough front-end reviews designed to prevent errors and misstatements. Based on our interviews and test work, it appears that program, field, and regional offices primarily analyze transactions and reports on budgetary execution. Asset and liability management and review of proprietary account information is primarily the responsibility of the Division of Finance. We also noted that the Service did not detect errors in its 2000 Annual Report prior to printing. These errors included certain material items, which were corrected through an "Errata Sheet" that the Service issued in October 2001.

Account Reconciliations. The Service did not perform regular account reconciliations and management reviews of various reconciliations at the Finance Center during the year. Specifically, we noted that:

- The Service did not perform reconciliations of propriety to budgetary accounts as well as suspense accounts at year end.

- The Service did not reconcile subsidiary financial records to the general ledger in a timely manner. For example, the Service reconciles property, plant, and equipment at year end only as discussed in our material weakness comments relating to capital equipment and buildings, structures, and construction work in process.

- The original draft of the Service's 2001 Statement of Financing did not fully reconcile to the Statement of Net Cost. This situation required an adjustment of approximately $15 million to properly reflect expended appropriations for capitalized assets. The Service also had other unreconciled differences.

- The Service was unable to fully reconcile its balances with other bureaus within the Department. This intradepartmental elimination process was also not performed in a timely manner.

Accrual Accounting. The Service did not properly accrue accounts payable. Based on our audit work the Service made an adjustment of approximately $18 million to properly reflect accounts

3

payable. The Service also did not accrue liabilities for goods and services provided under reimbursable agreements and the related accounts receivable totaling approximately $4 million. Also, the Service did not accrue the correct amount of its environmental cleanup liabilities. The Service determined that its accrued cleanup cost included 100% of the total cleanup costs of the site. Based on this information, the Service adjusted its estimated environmental liability by approximately $90 million to reflect only those cleanup costs that are probable to be paid by the Service.

Transaction Processing. The Service records certain material transactions only at year end. For some other material transactions, the Service does not record them in a timely manner throughout the year. Both of these situations require various reconciliations and entries in order to present accurate and complete financial results. We also noted that Service personnel coded numerous transactions to incorrect budget object classes (BOCs) which map to standard general ledger accounts. The BOCs track disbursements according to type such as, but not limited to, compensation, benefits, travel, purchase of goods and services from governmental agencies and equipment and structures. In many instances the Service corrected the original incorrect postings through its review or reconciliation processes; however, this practice is manually intensive and time consuming. Finally, the Service did not properly post certain transactions to Standard General Ledger (SGL) accounts during the year. For example, the Service made adjusting entries to expended appropriations for capitalized assets to properly close account balances at year end.

The deficiencies in the Service's financial reporting process result from:

- Inadequate or poorly designed controls and systems.

- Lack of appropriate training.

- Inadequate management oversight of financial transactions.

Accurate and timely financial information is critical to the Service's decision making process. As a result of the issues noted above, the financial reporting process is inefficient and, at times, erroneous. As a result, the Service's financial statements may be materially misstated and the Service may not detect the misstatements. Further, the Service may make erroneous decisions based on this financial information.

Recommendation

The Service should reevaluate its financial reporting process to improve its efficiency and effectiveness. The manual efforts currently required to generate financial statements should be taken into consideration. The Service's evaluation should include, but not be limited to:

- Reviewing Service policies and procedures to ensure that internal and external financial reporting is accurate, complete, and timely. This review should also evaluate current processes to utilize information technology systems and eliminate unnecessary effort.

- Reviewing the staffing and organizational structure of the financial reporting function to ensure accurate, complete, and timely financial reporting.

- Ensuring that account reconciliations are performed on a regular basis throughout the year with appropriate management review.

- Training Division of Finance, Program and Regional, and National Business Center personnel on transaction coding, account analysis, and financial reporting. This training should ensure that personnel are adequately trained on the Hyperion financial reporting application. The

4

Service should also enhance training of personnel responsible for coding and approving disbursements to ensure these transactions are coded to the proper BOC and SGLs at the initial transaction.

- Ensuring program and regional personnel properly accrue accounts receivable and payables at year end. Ensuring the Service properly assesses its probability of payment for environmental cleanup costs in determining its liability.

- Developing periodic review processes by program managers of Federal Financial System information, not limited to budgetary results.

Management Response

The Service generally agrees that the efficiency and effectiveness of its financial reporting process can be improved. The Service has already initiated several new internal controls and review processes to ensure that financial reporting is accurate and complete. This year we are moving toward more frequent reconciliations of key information systems with the Federal Financial System (FFS) to prepare quarterly financial statements. Actions taken or planned to address KPMG's recommendation's are:

- Review finance policies and procedures – We are currently evaluating key business and reporting processes, revising key financial management policies and guidance, and identifying areas requiring additional training and technical assistance to improve performance. Target Date: September 2002.

- Review staffing and organizational structure – There has been a dramatic increase in the scope and complexity of the Service's accounting and reporting requirements in recent years. Positions have been added to the Service's Finance Center. All existing vacancies are advertised and will be filled during FY 2002. Target Date: September 2002.

- Ensuring account reconciliations are performed regularly – As discussed above, the Service will incorporate clarifying guidance into FWS Manual releases, policies and directives to require more frequent reconciliations throughout the year. Target Date: September 2002.

- Training Service personnel in financial reporting – Training of personnel responsible for transaction processing, account analysis, and financial reporting function is a high priority for the Service. The National Conversation Training Center offers courses addressing financial management issues, which are regularly attended. The Service provides formal and informal training at all levels of the organization. Given these ongoing efforts to train Service personnel on accounting and reporting processes, there is little opportunity to enhance training efforts as recommended; however, we plan to reach a greater number of Service personnel outside the finance community. We are heightening recognition of training needs by updating financial management policies to clarify processes required and the roles and responsibilities of personnel involved with financial management functions. Target Date: September 2002.

- Ensuring Service personnel properly accrue accounts receivable and payables – Over the past several years, the Service has been adding detailed instructions to its year end guidance and will continue this year with further clarifications and improvements to address proper procedures for accrual transactions, including more complete considerations when estimating the Service's share of future environmental cleanup liabilities prior to making an accrual entry. Target Date: July 2002.

5

- Developing periodic review processes by program managers – A process for reviewing key financial management business practices performed at field stations is being developed this year. The process will identify those field stations and/or Regions where more focused guidance or training is needed to ensure the accuracy, timeliness and reliability of proprietary, as well as budgetary, financial information. Target Date: August 2002.

B. Controls, Processes, and Financial Reporting Relating to Capital Equipment

The Service needs to improve its controls and processes associated with the accounting for and reporting of capital equipment. During our audit, we noted the following:

- Each region uses a different property system to account for capital equipment. The Finance Center uses an Excel spreadsheet to support the capital equipment balances in the accounting records and financial statements. The Finance Center updates the spreadsheet twice a year for additions and once a year for disposals, based on information that the regions submit.

- Several reconciliations are performed between the Excel spreadsheet and the accounting records. The Service reconciles property systems to the Federal Financial System (FFS) support by amount only and does not compare property numbers or other information. This situation could lead to inaccurate entries made to FFS.

- The Service records corrections to capital equipment through current year activity without an evaluation as to the impact to prior year recorded amounts.

- The Service did not properly reflect the acquisition cost of capital equipment transferred to the Service from other federal agencies. The Service recorded transferred equipment at the original acquisition value instead of fair value or net book value.

- Each region (specifically Office of Contracting and General Services) prepares a monthly property reconciliation form, which is submitted to the Finance Center to update FFS. The form contains a section for reconciliation to the general ledger. FFS does not maintain detailed property information by region on a monthly basis. The general ledger balances on the form are rolled forward each month from the prior reconciliation. As a result, the current reconciliation form is not accurate.

- Each region performs an annual physical inventory of capital equipment as of October 1. The Service requires field offices to submit the inventory results to the regional office by mid-December. Although the inventory is taken as of year end, the Finance Center does not make any adjustments to the year end financial statements based on the results.

- The Service recorded depreciation expense for some equipment acquired prior to March 31st. This is inconsistent with Service policy. Also, the Service calculates depreciation only at year end.

The Service does not have adequate controls over financial reporting of capital equipment. As a result, the Service's process for financial reporting is manually intensive, accumulating information from numerous sources and systems. As a result of the number of systems used and the amount of manually intensive work involved, the Service's processes are inefficient. Also, capital equipment may be misstated in the financial statements based on the Service's timing and accuracy of financial reporting, depreciation policies, and timing of annual inventories.

6

Recommendation

We understand that the Service is currently assessing its capital equipment processes. We recommend the Service continue these efforts to evaluate its processes for acquiring, tracking, and reporting capital equipment. Specifically, the Service should:

- Evaluate current processes to utilize information technology systems and eliminate unnecessary effort.

- Consider using one property system for the Regional Offices and the Finance Center for capital equipment.

- Work towards quarterly reporting of capital equipment. Specifically, the Service should post acquisitions and dispositions for all capital equipment, as well as depreciation to FFS on a periodic basis throughout the year. Ensure depreciation policies are consistently applied.

- Ensure any corrections to prior year capital equipment are properly evaluated as potential prior period adjustments.

- Record capital equipment transferred balances from other agencies at net book value not original acquisition cost.

- Modify regional property reconciliations to streamline the process and provide the Finance Center necessary information.

- Reevaluate the timing of annual physical inventories considering financial reporting requirements.

Management Response

The Service recognizes that the processes governing the reporting of accurate information regarding capitalized equipment could be improved. Last year, the Service established a Capitalized Equipment Workgroup (CEW) to address specific audit findings regarding the Service's FY 2000 financial statements. The work of the CEW continues this year. Below are detailed actions taken or planned to implement KPMG's recommendations:

- Use one property system for capitalized equipment – The Service has identified a candidate for a Service-wide system and is currently developing an implementation plan. Target Date: June 2002.

- Work toward quarterly reporting, with appropriate application of depreciation policies – Depreciation relating to capital equipment will be updated in FFS to coincide with quarterly reports and policy and procedures for recording capital equipment in FFS will be reviewed and revised as necessary to ensure that capital equipment is reported accurately in FFS. This process will also be applied to reporting on buildings, structures, and construction work-in-progress, as outlined in C, below. Target Date: July 2002.

- Evaluate corrections to prior year capital equipment – The Service will review and revise, as necessary, processes for correcting prior year capital equipment transactions so that the impact of corrections on prior year recorded amounts are recognized and appropriate prior year adjustments are made. Target Date: September 2002.

- Record capital equipment at net book value – Service policies and procedures governing the recording to transferred capital equipment will be evaluated and revised, as necessary, to ensure that transfers are recorded at net book value. Target Date: June 2002.

7

- Modify and streamline Regional property reconciliations – The Service is reviewing its property management processes and systems to facilitate monthly and quarterly reconciliations with FFS. Also, the Service will review processes to evaluate whether proper information is being exchanged timely. Target Date: August 2002.

- Evaluate the timing of annual inventories – The Service will re-evaluate the timing of annual physical inventories to assess the impacts of current schedules and whether a change is necessary to ensure timely submission of information for financial statement reporting of personal property inventory. Target Date: July 2002.

C. **Controls, Processes, and Financial Reporting Relating to Buildings, Structures, and Construction Work in Process**

The Service needs to improve its controls and processes associated with the accounting for and reporting of buildings, structures and construction work in process (CWIP). During our audit, we noted the following:

- The Service only records certain adjustments to the official Property, Plant, and Equipment (PP&E) accounting records semi-annually for buildings and structures, and construction work in process. The Service records depreciation only at year end. Further, the Service only records adjustments to the official accounting records for land at year end.

- The Service's Regional Offices and the Finance Center use the Real Property Inventory (RPI) system, a separate system from FFS, to track buildings and structures. Service personnel perform an intensive, manual reconciliation twice a year to accumulate accurate and complete financial data for construction work in process, buildings, and structures. The Finance Center uses an Excel spreadsheet to support the buildings and structures balance in the financial statements. The Finance Center updates the spreadsheet twice a year with additions and disposals.

- The Service did not complete its CWIP review in a timely manner in fiscal year 2001. As a result, there was a delay in the Service's financial reporting process. We also noted errors in the Service's evaluation of asset capitalization and expense.

- The Service reused property numbers in RPI for new acquisitions that replaced existing facilities. This caused errors in depreciation expense.

- The Service changed the useful lives and acquisition dates of certain buildings and structures. Some changes were made in error and others were made to correct errors in the RPI system. The Service did not evaluate the effect of these changes on prior period recorded amounts. However, for at least the third straight year, the Service did make other prior period adjustments to buildings and structures in fiscal year 2001.

- The Service assigns a useful life of 30 years to all buildings and structures regardless of location, function, or type of construction.

- The Service depreciates building improvements over 30 years as opposed to the remaining useful life of the related structure.

The Service does not have an adequate financial reporting system for buildings, structures, and CWIP. As a result, the Service's process for financial reporting is manually intensive, accumulating information from numerous sources and systems. As a result of the number of systems used and the amount of manually intensive work involved, the Service's processes in this area are inefficient.

8

Also, these assets may be misstated in the financial statements based on the Service's timing of financial reporting, useful lives of assets, and depreciation policies.

Recommendation

The Service should:

- Evaluate current buildings, structures, and CWIP processes to streamline efforts, ensure timely information is available for financial reporting and eliminate misstatements.

- Work towards quarterly reporting of buildings, structures, and CWIP. Specifically, the Service should post acquisitions and dispositions for all buildings, structures, and CWIP, as well as depreciation, to FFS on a periodic basis throughout the year.

- Train Regional Offices on the use of RPI, specifically focusing on the reuse of property numbers and changes to acquisition dates.

- Evaluate the useful lives of buildings and structures to ensure appropriateness given the expected use of the assets.

- Change the useful life of building improvements to the remaining useful life of the related structure.

- Ensure leasehold improvements are evaluated for capitalization.

Management Response

This recommendation crosses several operational areas of responsibility within the Service at all levels of the organization. Completing these recommendations will require a coordinated effort of the entire Directorate, with focused leadership from the Service's Refuge and Fish Hatchery Programs. Actions taken or planned to address KPMG's recommendations are:

- Evaluate processes to streamline efforts and ensure that real property information is timely and accurate – Improved maintenance of property is high priority of the Service and the Department and considerable improvements have been made to enhance the reliability of property information. The Service plans to amend the Real Property Inventory (RPI) database to generate a report that identifies the mechanisms through which assets were either acquired or disposed and the additions to the RPI resulting from the conduct of condition assessments. Target Date: September 2002.

  The Service will review and streamline CWIP processes to increase efficiencies through automated processes: Target Date: July 2002.

- Work toward quarterly reporting – The Service needs to establish processes and procedures to accomplish quarterly reporting of information pertinent to the management of buildings, structures, and CWIP. Our commitment will build from revisions made to the RPI database, changes made to existing reconciliation processes, and guidance from the Department on appropriate reporting of quarterly amounts and balances related to buildings, structures, and CWIP. This process will be coordinated with reporting on capitalized equipment, as outlined in B above. Target Date: July 2002.

- Train personnel on the use of the RPI – The Service recognizes that the reuse of old property numbers and unsubstantiated changes to acquisition dates need to be avoided. We will lock database fields, refine user instructions, and complete additional training. Target Date: September 2002.

9

- Evaluate useful lives of buildings and structures, including remaining useful of building improvements – We will refine the criteria for calculating the useful life of buildings, including the remaining useful life of building improvements. The Service will use the revised criteria to allocate improvement funds, report accomplishments, and determine proper accounting treatments. Target Date: September 2002.

- Evaluate leasehold improvements for capitalization – The Service will evaluate existing policy and provide clarifying guidance to implement this suggestion. Target Date: July 2002.

D. Security and General Controls Over Financial Management Systems

Despite the fact that the Service has made recent improvements in the security and controls over its information systems, controls need to be improved in the areas described below, as required by OMB Circular A-130, *Management of Federal Information Resources*. These conditions could affect the Service's ability to prevent and detect unauthorized changes to financial information, control electronic access to sensitive information, and protect its information resources.

Entity-wide Security Program and Planning: An entity-wide security program, including security policies and a related implementation plan, is the foundation of an entity's security control structure and a reflection of senior management's commitment to addressing security risks. As outlined in OMB Circular A-130, an effective security program includes a risk assessment process, a certification process, and an effective incident response and monitoring capability. The Service does not have a comprehensive entity-wide security plan, which identifies established security plans, security program management and related personnel, as well as ongoing management of security policies and procedures. Specifically, the Service has not:

- Performed comprehensive entity-wide risk assessments of its general support systems and major applications systems and reviewed these assessments for accuracy and completeness.

- Finalized and implemented comprehensive security policies to include the establishment of a security management structure and clearly assigned security responsibilities.

- Established consistent security-related personnel policies and procedures.

- Established and enforced entity-wide computer security training.

Access Controls: Access controls should provide reasonable assurance that computer resources (data files, application programs, and computer-related facilities and equipment) are protected against unauthorized modification, disclosure, loss, or impairment. The objectives of limiting access are to ensure that: (1) users have only the access needed to perform their duties; (2) access to very sensitive resources, such as security software programs, is limited to very few individuals; and (3) employees are restricted from performing incompatible functions or functions beyond their responsibilities. The Service did not have adequate controls to limit or detect access to certain information systems in order to protect against unauthorized modification, loss and disclosure of data. We noted:

- Lack of adherence to the Service's policy for maintaining individual user accounts.

- Weak access controls and password management for the network and remote field stations.

- Weaknesses with network security through configuration management.

- Need for a Service-wide policy for routine revalidation of users to general support systems and specific applications.

10

- Weak internal access authentication.

- Need for entity-wide password administration standards.

- Need for continued implementation of firewalls and configuration of standard rules.

Software Development and Change Controls: Establishing controls over the modification of application software programs help to ensure that only authorized programs and authorized modifications are implemented. Without proper controls, there is a risk that security features could be inadvertently or deliberately omitted or "turned-off," or that processing irregularities could be introduced. The Service has not fully developed procedures for controlling changes over application software that would prevent unauthorized programs or modifications to an existing program from being implemented. In addition, duties are not properly segregated as application programmers responsible for making changes over application software also approve these changes and move them to production.

System Software Controls: Controls over the modification of system software change controls should provide reasonable assurance that operating system controls are not compromised. Without proper system software controls, unauthorized individuals using the system software could circumvent controls to read, modify, or delete critical or sensitive information or programs. The Service has not fully established system software controls that limit and monitor access to the programs and sensitive files that control the computer hardware and secure applications supported by the system. The Service has not fully developed procedures to ensure that tests of system software changes are performed and documented, system software changes are reviewed, approval is documented before implementation, and duties are properly segregated.

Segregation of Duties: Segregation of duties is important to ensure the division of roles and responsibilities and steps in critical functions are designed in information systems so that no one individual can undermine the process. We noted weaknesses in the Service's segregation of duties for its information systems, specifically relating to:

- Policies and procedures governing the identification, assignment, and monitoring of National Communications Center (NCC) information functions.

- Policies addressing incompatible duties access.

- Job functions between security and systems administration and application programming functions.

Service Continuity: Losing the capability to process, retrieve, and protect information maintained electronically could significantly impact the Service's ability to accomplish its mission. Thus, procedures should be in place to protect information resources, minimize the risk of unplanned interruptions, and recover critical operations should interruptions occur. To mitigate the risk of service interruptions, the Service needs to improve its Service-wide Continuity of Operations Plans so that critical systems are prioritized, responsibilities are clearly assigned, alternate processing is clearly identified, restoration of critical functions is addressed, and the plans have been tested.

National Business Center: The Department of the Interior National Business Center (NBC) administers several of the Service's financial management systems, including: the Federal Personnel and Payroll System (FPPS), Federal Financial System (FFS), Hyperion, and the Interior Department Electronic Acquisitions System (IDEAS). Although NBC has recently improved the security and controls over these information systems, NBC needs to continue improvements in the areas of: entity-wide security planning, configuration of operating systems, system software controls, software development and change controls, and service continuity. Weaknesses in these control areas could

11

affect the Service's ability to prevent and detect unauthorized changes to its financial information and increases the Service's need for less efficient manual controls to monitor and reconcile financial information.

Recommendation

We recommend that the Service develop and implement a formal action plan to improve the security and general controls over the financial management systems. This plan should address each of the areas discussed above, as well as other areas that might impact the EDP control environment to ensure adequate security and protection of the Service's financial management systems. We also recommend that the Service annually obtain appropriate assurance (similar to a SAS 70 Type II report) from the NBC that adequate security and controls are in place over the financial management systems the NBC administers.

Management Response

While the Service agrees with the general finding that controls need to be improved in the areas indicated by KPMG, we disagree that there is sufficient risk to endanger financial management statements or operations. Plans to improve controls are underway and will occur in two phases. In the first phase, policies and guidelines relating to IT security are being revised to address the cited areas of weakness. Target Date: July 2002.

During the second phase, programs and Regions cited during the audit will be monitored to ensure corrective actions are being taken to bring their operations into compliance with new policies. Target Date: September 2002.

Although the Service is not in a position to address the finding regarding the National Business Center (NBC), the Service agrees to secure from NBC appropriate assurances regarding the adequacy of their security and controls in place over the systems they administer. Target Date: July 2002.

We noted the following reportable condition that is not considered to be a material weakness:

E. Financial Reporting of the Sport Fish Restoration Account

Title 26 USC Section 9504 establishes the Aquatic Resources Trust Fund (ARTF) and authorizes the transfer of certain taxes received by the Department of Treasury. Appropriations are made from the ARTF to two accounts: the Service's Sport Fish Restoration Account (SFRA) and the Boat Safety Account (BSA) of the United States Coast Guard (Coast Guard).

We noted that the Service recorded budget authority for the SFRA based on appropriation transfers from Treasury on the SF-1151. According to public law, the SFRA, reported in the Service's budget, was appropriated approximately $417 million in fiscal year 2001 and was to make appropriation transfers to the Corps of Engineers and Coast Guard of approximately $117 million. In fiscal year 2001 only $81.1 million was drawn down by the Corps of Engineers and Coast Guard. Although the flow of funds via Treasury's SF-1151 indicated the Service itself drew down approximately $295 million, the Service should have recorded the full appropriation of $417 million in its financial records and corresponding appropriation transfers of $81.1 million.

In accordance with Statement of Federal Financial Accounting Standard No. 7, *Accounting for Revenue and Other Financing Sources,* and Statement of Federal Financial Accounting Concepts Number 2, *Entity and Display*, beginning in fiscal year 2001, the ARTF is recorded in the financial statements of the Service. While the Service obtains a majority of the financial information from the Treasury's Bureau of Public Debt to record the ARTF, it should also record the SFRA budget

12

authority and cash draws in order to accurately and completely reflect amounts due to other program agencies.

We noted the three different Divisions within the Service (the Division of Budget, Division of Federal Aid, and Division of Finance) record the SFRA budget authority and two Divisions record cash draws. These three Divisions' amounts for the difference between budget authority and cash drawn did not agree. Also, the Service could not initially provide supporting documentation for the $400 million SFRA receivable in its financial records which represented monies undrawn from the SFRA by the Service. The Service did reconcile this receivable to its underlying accounting records.

The Service recorded the ARTF in its financial statements for the first time in fiscal year 2001 and did not have adequate communication between the Division of Budget, Division of Federal Aid and Division of Finance regarding account balances of SFRA. In order to fairly present its financial statements, the Service should ensure that the appropriate information is available to record the ARTF and that the SFRA appropriation is properly recorded.

Recommendation

The Service should implement policies and procedures to ensure transactions relating to the ARTF and SFRA are accurately and completely reported in the Federal Financial System and its financial statements. These policies and procedures should include:

- Completing the Memorandum of Understanding between the Service and applicable agencies relating to SFRA. The Memorandum should ensure that information is available to properly record the ARTF in the financial statements of the Service in a timely manner.

- Ensuring adequate communication is made between the Service's Division of Budget, Division of Federal Aid, and Division of Finance regarding to the completeness and accuracy of the SFRA account balances, including remaining budget authority of the Service, Corps of Engineers, and Coast Guard.

- Recording, in accordance with the federal budget, the SFRA appropriation and related appropriation transfers to the Corps of Engineers and Coast Guard.

Management Response

This year was the first year for reporting the ARTF. The Memorandum of Understanding (MOU) being drafted will seek to clarify the roles and responsibilities of the Service, the U.S. Coast Guard, and the Corps of Engineers. Approval of the MOU is the responsibility of the Office of Management and Budget and the Department of the Treasury. The MOU will identify the specific responsibilities of the Bureau of Public Debt in the Department of the Treasury to make monthly and periodic reports available to the Service and other program agencies regarding financial activity of the ARTF. Full implementation of this recommendation will require the coordinated participation of all agencies responsible for managing and expending ARTF funds. Target Date: September 2002.

A summary of the status of prior year reportable conditions is included as Exhibit I. We also noted other matters involving the internal control over financial reporting and its operation that we have reported to the management of the Service in a separate letter dated January 21, 2002.

Compliance With Laws and Regulations

The results of our tests of compliance with the laws and regulations described in the responsibilities section of this report, exclusive of FFMIA, disclosed no instances of noncompliance that are required to be reported herein under *Government Auditing Standards* or OMB Bulletin No. 01-02, *Audit Requirements for Federal Financial Statements*.

13

The results of our tests of FFMIA disclosed instances, described below, where the Service's financial management systems did not substantially comply with Federal financial management systems requirements and Federal accounting standards.

F.   Financial Management Systems Requirements

As discussed in the section of our report entitled, *Internal Control over Financial Reporting*, the Service needs to improve its EDP security and general control environment. As a result, the Service does not substantially comply with the EDP security and general control requirements of OMB Circular A-130, *Management of Federal Information Resources*.

Recommendation

We recommend that the Service take the necessary actions to improve security and general controls over its financial management systems in accordance with requirements set forth in OMB Circular A-130 in fiscal year 2002.

Management Response

The Service has made substantial efforts with limited resources to comply with OMB Circular A-130 and acknowledges that it needs to make improvements. The Service believes that the actions outlined in our response to finding D, in the Internal Control over Financial Reporting section will correct the issues that led to this finding.

G.   Federal Accounting Standards

The Service is required to prepare its financial statements in accordance with Federal accounting standards. As discussed in the section of this report entitled, *Internal Control over Financial Reporting*, we identified material weaknesses that affected the Service's ability to prepare its financial statements and related disclosures in accordance with Federal accounting standards. The foregoing material weaknesses in internal control are also an indicator of noncompliance with FFMIA provisions relating to Federal accounting standards.

Recommendation

We recommend that the Service strengthen its procedures and internal control to ensure that its financial statements and related disclosures are prepared in accordance with Federal accounting standards.

Management Response

The Service acknowledges that its processes for preparing its financial statements and related disclosures can be improved. The Service believes that the actions outlined in our responses to the findings in the Internal Control over Financial Reporting section will correct the issues that led to this finding.

The results of our tests disclosed no instances in which the Service did not substantially comply with the United States Government Standard General Ledger at the transaction level.

Responsibilities

Management's Responsibility

The Government Management Reform Act of 1994 (GMRA) requires federal agency's to report annually to Congress on its financial status and any other information needed to fairly present its financial position and results of operations. To meet the GMRA reporting requirements, the Service prepares annual financial statements.

14

Management is responsible for:

- Preparing the financial statements in conformity with accounting principles generally accepted in the United States of America;

- Establishing and maintaining internal controls over financial reporting, required supplementary stewardship information, and performance measures; and

- Complying with laws and regulations, including FFMIA.

In fulfilling this responsibility, estimates and judgments by management are required to assess the expected benefits and related costs of internal control policies.

Auditors' Responsibility

Our responsibility is to express an opinion on the fiscal year 2001 financial statements of the Service based on our audit. We conducted our audit in accordance with auditing standards generally accepted in the United States of America, the standards applicable to financial audits contained in *Government Auditing Standards*, issued by the Comptroller General of the United States, and OMB Bulletin No. 01-02. Those standards and OMB Bulletin No. 01-02 require that we plan and perform the audit to obtain reasonable assurance about whether the financial statements are free of material misstatement.

An audit includes:

- Examining, on a test basis, evidence supporting the amounts and disclosures in the financial statements;

- Assessing the accounting principles used and significant estimates made by management; and

- Evaluating the overall financial statement presentation.

We believe that our audit provides a reasonable basis for our opinion.

In planning and performing our fiscal year 2001 audit, we considered the Service's internal control over financial reporting by obtaining an understanding of the Service's internal control, determining whether internal controls had been placed in operation, assessing control risk, and performing tests of controls in order to determine our auditing procedures for the purpose of expressing our opinion on the financial statements. We limited our internal control testing to those controls necessary to achieve the objectives described in OMB Bulletin No. 01-02 and *Government Auditing Standards*. We did not test all internal controls relevant to operating objectives as broadly defined by the Federal Managers' Financial Integrity Act of 1982. The objective of our audit was not to provide assurance on internal controls over financial reporting. Consequently, we do not provide an opinion on internal control over financial reporting.

As required by OMB Bulletin No. 01-02, we considered the Service's internal control over Required Supplementary Stewardship Information by obtaining an understanding of the Service's internal control, determining whether these internal controls had been placed in operation, assessing control risk, and performing tests of controls. Our procedures were not designed to provide assurance on internal control over Required Supplementary Stewardship Information and, accordingly, we do not provide an opinion on such controls.

As further required by OMB Bulletin No. 01-02, with respect to internal control related to performance measures determined by management to be key and reported in the Supplementary Information on Service Performance and financial highlights of Service Financial Performance, we obtained an understanding of the design of significant internal controls relating to the existence and completeness assertions. Our procedures were not designed to provide assurance on internal control over performance measures and, accordingly, we do not provide an opinion on such controls.

15

As part of obtaining reasonable assurance about whether the Service's fiscal year 2001 financial statements are free of material misstatement, we performed tests of the Service's compliance with certain provisions of laws and regulations, noncompliance with which could have a direct and material effect on the determination of financial statement amounts, and certain provisions of other laws and regulations specified in OMB Bulletin No. 01-02, including certain provisions referred to in FFMIA. We limited our tests of compliance to the provisions described in the preceding sentence, and we did not test compliance with all laws and regulations applicable to the Service. Providing an opinion on compliance with laws and regulations was not an objective of our audit, and, accordingly, we do not express such an opinion.

Under FFMIA, we are required to report whether the Service's financial management systems substantially comply with: (1) Federal financial management systems requirements, (2) applicable Federal accounting standards, and (3) the United States Government Standard General Ledger at the transaction level. To meet this requirement, we performed tests of compliance with FFMIA section 803(a) requirements.

Distribution

This report is intended for the information and use of United States Fish and Wildlife Service management, Department of the Interior, Department of the Interior's Office of the Inspector General, OMB, and the U.S. Congress, and is not intended to be and should not be used by anyone other than these specified parties.

January 21, 2002

16

United States Department of the Interior

Office of Inspector General
Washington, D.C. 20240

Independent Auditors' Report

To: Acting Director, U.S. Fish and Wildlife Service

Subject: U.S. Fish and Wildlife Service's Financial Statements for Fiscal Year 2000

We have audited the U.S. Fish and Wildlife Service's (FWS) consolidated balance sheet and related notes as of September 30, 2000. The objective of our audit was to express an opinion on the fair presentation of the consolidated balance sheet. This financial statement is the responsibility of the FWS, and our responsibility is to express an opinion, based on our audit, on this financial statement.

We conducted our audit in accordance with the auditing standards generally accepted in the United States of America; the standards for financial audits contained in *Government Auditing Standards*, issued by the Comptroller General of the United States; and with Office of Management and Budget (OMB) Bulletin No. 01-02, *Audit Requirements for Federal Financial Statements*. These standards and OMB Bulletin No. 01-02 require that we plan and perform our audit to obtain reasonable assurance as to whether the accompanying consolidated balance sheet and related notes are free of material misstatement. An audit includes examining, on a test basis, evidence supporting the amounts and disclosures contained in the consolidated balance sheet and the accompanying notes. An audit also includes assessing the accounting principles used and the significant estimates made by management, as well as evaluating the overall consolidated balance sheet presentation. We believe that our audit of the consolidated balance sheet provides a reasonable basis for our opinion.

In our opinion, the consolidated balance sheet referred to above presents fairly, in all material respects, the financial position of the FWS as of September 30, 2000 in conformity with accounting principles generally accepted in the United States of America.

As discussed in Notes 16 to the financial statements, the FWS restated its previously reported consolidated statement of financial position (balance sheet) amounts for corrections related to depreciation of buildings and structures and grantee expenses, and for a change in its reporting policies to include the Aquatic Resources Trust Fund in its statements (see also Note 15).

In our report dated February 14, 2001, we expressed an opinion that FWS' statement of net cost for the year ended September 30, 2000 presented fairly, in all material respects, it's net cost of operations in conformity with accounting principles generally accepted in the United States of America. As described in Note 1M, FWS has restated its statement of net cost for the year ended September 30, 2000 to conform with the presentation of net cost for the year ended September 30, 2001. We did not audit the restated statement of net cost for the year ended September 30, 2000, and accordingly, we do not express an opinion on this statement and related notes.

Roger La Rouche
Assistant Inspector General for Audits
February 14, 2001, except for Notes 15 and 16
as to which the date is January 11, 2002

United States Department of the Interior

FISH AND WILDLIFE SERVICE
Washington, D.C. 20240

In Reply Refer To:
FWS/DF

FEB 2 1 2002

Memorandum

To: Curtis W. Crider
           Director of Financial Audits
           Office of Inspector General

From: Director *Steve Williams*

Subject: Draft Independent Auditors Report on the U.S. Fish and Wildlife Service's
           Financial Statements for Fiscal Years 2001 and 2000
           (Assignment No. C-IN-FWS-0048-2001)

The Service reviewed the subject draft audit report in which KPMG, LLP issued an unqualified opinion on the Service's financial statements for FY 2001. In this review, the Service reiterates its general agreement with KPMG findings and provides information on actions taken or planned to implement recommendations. However, the Service disagrees with the finding on compliance with laws and regulations and provides the basis for our conclusion. The Service appreciates its review comments being incorporated into the final audit report.

For FY 2000, the Service appreciates receiving the OIG's opinion that the restated consolidated balance sheet and related notes as of September 30, 2000, are presented fairly in all material respects. We will cross-reference the Service's restatement and the resultant findings by the OIG regarding the Service's FY 2000 financial statements in the Service's FY 2000 Annual Report entitled, "Shared Commitments to Conservation."

General Comments

Many of the recommendations from KPMG ask the Service to evaluate current processes and use information technology (IT) systems to streamline efforts and to reduce manual reconciliations of subsidiary information systems with the core financial system, the Federal Financial System (FFS). We agree that timely reporting relies on advances achieved in using IT systems and recently completed an electronic interface between the FFS and the Federal Aid Information Management System (FAIMS) which is yielding timely reports and assuring reporting accuracy of grants management actions. However, we are cautious in our efforts to develop new systems or interfaces for two reasons. First, the Department of the Interior has underway a Systems Migration Project to

1

develop a comprehensive administrative system that would include integrated financial accounting and fixed asset modules. If we develop a comprehensive, unified Service financial management system, it is likely that it could be replaced within a short time by a Departmental system. Second, there is no established IT architecture for the Department, which increases the difficulty of efficiently developing new systems.

Report on Internal Controls

A. Improve Financial Reporting Process

The Service generally agrees that the efficiency and effectiveness of its financial reporting process can be improved. The Service has already initiated several new internal controls and review processes to ensure that financial reporting is accurate and complete. This year we are moving toward more frequent reconciliations of key information systems with FFS to prepare quarterly financial statements.

For the following actions taken or planned to address KPMG recommendations, the Service's Lead Official for establishing policies and operational guidelines is the Assistant Director - Business Management and Operations and Implementing Officials are all Assistant and Regional Directors:

- Review finance policies and procedures - We are currently evaluating key business and reporting processes, revising key financial management policies and guidance, and identifying areas requiring additional training and technical assistance to improve performance. Target Date: September 2002

- Review staffing and organizational structure - There has been a dramatic increase in the scope and complexity of the Service's accounting and reporting requirements in recent years. Positions have been added to the Service's Finance Center. All existing vacancies are advertised and will be filled during FY 2002. Target Date: September 2002

- Ensuring account reconciliations are performed regularly - As discussed above, the Service will incorporate clarifying guidance into FWS Manual releases, policies and directives to require more frequent reconciliations throughout the year. Target Date: September 2002

- Training Service personnel in financial reporting - Training of personnel responsible for transaction processing, account analysis and financial reporting function is a high priority for the Service. The National Conservation Training Center offers courses addressing financial management issues, which are regularly attended. The Service provides formal and informal training at all levels of the organization. Given these ongoing efforts to train Service personnel on accounting and reporting processes, there is little opportunity to enhance training efforts as recommended; however, we plan to reach a greater number of Service personnel outside the finance community. We are heightening recognition of training needs by updating financial management policies to clarify processes required and the roles and

2

responsibilities of personnel involved with financial management functions. Target Date: September 2002

- Ensuring Service personnel properly accrue accounts receivable and payables - Over the past several years, the Service has been adding detailed instructions to its year end guidance and will continue this year with further clarifications and improvements to address proper procedures for accrual transactions, including more complete considerations when estimating the Service's share of future environmental cleanup liabilities prior to making an accrual entry. Target Date: July 2002

- Developing periodic review processes by program managers - A process for reviewing key financial management business practices performed at field stations is being developed this year. The process will identify those field stations and/or Regions where more focused guidance or training is needed to ensure the accuracy, timeliness and reliability of proprietary, as well as budgetary, financial information. Target Date: August 2002

B. Improve Controls, Processes and Financial Reporting Relating to Capital Equipment

The Service recognizes that the processes governing the reporting of accurate information regarding capitalized equipment could be improved. Last year, the Service established a Capitalized Equipment Workgroup (CEW) to address specific audit findings regarding the Service's FY 2000 financial statements. The work of the CEW continues this year. Below are detailed actions taken or planned to implement KPMG recommendations:

- Use one property system for capitalized equipment - The Service has identified a candidate for a Service-wide system and is currently developing an implementation plan. Target date: June 2002. Responsible Official: Chief, Division of Contracting and General Services

- Work toward quarterly reporting, with appropriate application of depreciation policies - Depreciation relating to capital equipment will be updated in FFS to coincide with quarterly reports and policy and procedures for recording capital equipment in FFS will be reviewed and revised as necessary to ensure that capital equipment is reported accurately in FFS. This process will also be applied to reporting on buildings, structures and construction work-in-progress, as outlined in C. below. Target Date: July 2002. Policy Co-Lead: Chief, Division of Finance and Chief, Division of Contracting and General Services and Implementation Leads: Chief, Division of Contracting and General Services for personal property, Chief, Division of Engineering for CWIP, and Chief, National Wildlife Refuges for RPI, with Chief, Division of Finance providing accounting expertise

- Evaluate corrections to prior year capital equipment - The Service will review and revise, as necessary, processes for correcting prior year capital equipment transactions so that the

3

impact of corrections on prior year recorded amounts are recognized and appropriate prior year adjustments are made. Target Date: September 2002. Responsible Official: Chief, Division of Finance

- Record capital equipment at net book value - Service policies and procedures governing the recording of transferred capital equipment will be evaluated and revised, as necessary, to ensure that transfers are recorded at net book value. Target Date: June 2002. Policy Lead: Chief, Division of Finance and Implementation Lead: Regional Directors

- Modify and streamline Regional property reconciliations - The Service is reviewing its property management processes and systems to facilitate monthly and quarterly reconciliations with FFS. Also, the Service will review processes to evaluate whether proper information is being exchanged timely. Target Date: August 2002. Responsible Officials: Chief, Division of Finance and Chief, Division of Contracting and General Services

- Evaluate the timing of annual inventories - The Service will re-evaluate the timing of annual physical inventories to assess the impacts of current schedules and whether a change is necessary to ensure timely submission of information for financial statement reporting of personal property inventory. Target Date: July 2002. Responsible Official: Chief, Division of Contracting and General Services

C. Improve Controls, Processes and Financial Reporting Relating to Buildings, Structures, and Construction Work in Progress (CWIP)

This recommendation crosses several operational areas of responsibility within the Service at all levels of the organization. Completing these recommendations will require a coordinated effort of the entire Directorate, with focused leadership from the Service's Refuge and Fish Hatchery Programs. For the following actions taken or planned to address KPMG recommendations, the Service will rely on the Co-Leadership of the Chief, National Wildlife Refuge System and the Assistant Director - Fisheries and Habitat Conservation, with the Assistant Director - Business Management and Operations providing accounting and technical engineering support:

- Evaluate processes to streamline efforts and ensure that real property information is timely and accurate - Improved maintenance of property is a high priority of the Service and the Department and considerable improvements have been made to enhance the reliability of property information. The Service plans to amend the Real Property Inventory (RPI) database to generate a report that identifies the mechanisms through which assets were either acquired or disposed and the additions to the RPI resulting from the conduct of condition assessments. Target Date: September 2002

  The Service will review and streamline CWIP processes to increase efficiencies through automated processes. Target Date: July 2002

4

- Work toward quarterly reporting - The Service needs to establish processes and procedures to accomplish quarterly reporting of information pertinent to the management of buildings, structures and CWIP. Our commitment will build from revisions made to the RPI database, changes made to existing reconciliation processes, and guidance from the Department on appropriate reporting of quarterly amounts and balances related to buildings, structures and CWIP. This process will be coordinated with reporting on capitalized equipment, as outlined in B. above. Target Date: July 2002. Implementation Leads: Chief, Division of Contracting and General Services for personal property, Chief, Division of Engineering for CWIP, and Chief, National Wildlife Refuges for RPI, with Chief, Division of Finance providing accounting expertise

- Train personnel on the use of the RPI - The Service recognizes that the reuse of old property numbers and unsubstantiated changes to acquisition dates need to be avoided. We will lock database fields, refine user instructions, and complete additional training. Target Date: September 2002

- Evaluate useful lives of buildings and structures, including remaining useful life of building improvements - We will refine the criteria for calculating the useful life of buildings, including the remaining useful life of building improvements. The Service will use the revised criteria to allocate improvement funds, report accomplishments, and determine proper accounting treatments. Target Date: September 2002

- Evaluate leasehold improvements for capitalization - The Service will evaluate existing policy and provide clarifying guidance to implement this suggestion. Target Date: July 2002. Responsible Official: Chief, Division of Contracting and General Services, in consultation with Chief, Division of Finance

D. Improve Security and General Controls Over Financial Management Systems

While the Service agrees with the general finding that controls need to be improved in the areas indicated by KPMG, we disagree that there is sufficient risk to endanger financial management statements or operations. Plans to improve controls are underway and will occur in two phases. In the first phase, policies and guidelines relating to IT security are being revised to address the cited areas of weakness. Target Date: July 2002. Responsible Official: Chief, Division of Information Resources Management

During the second phase, programs and Regions cited during the audit will be monitored to ensure corrective actions are being taken to bring their operations into compliance with new policies. Target Date: September 2002. Policy Official: Assistant Director for Business Management and Operations and Implementing Officials: All Assistant and Regional Directors

5

Although the Service is not in a position to address the finding regarding the National Business Center (NBC), the Service agrees to secure from NBC appropriate assurances regarding the adequacy of their security and controls in place over the systems they administer. Target Date: July 2002. Responsible Official: Chief, Division of Information Resources Management

E.   Improve Controls Over Financial Reporting of the Sport Fish Restoration Account (SFRA)

This year was the first year for reporting the Aquatic Resources Trust Fund (ARTF). The Memorandum of Understanding (MOU) being drafted will seek to clarify the roles and responsibilities of the Service, the U.S. Coast Guard and the Corps of Engineers. Approval of the MOU is the responsibility of the Office of Management and Budget and the Department of the Treasury. The MOU will identify the specific responsibilities of the Bureau of Public Debt in the Department of the Treasury to make monthly and periodic reports available to the Service and other program agencies regarding financial activity of the ARTF. Full implementation of this recommendation will require the coordinated participation of all agencies responsible for managing and expending ARTF funds. Target Date: September 2002. Policy Official: Assistant Director - Budget, Planning and Human Resources, with accounting assistance provided by the Assistant Director - Business Management and Operations and technical assistance provided by the Assistant Director - Migratory Birds and State Programs

Report on Compliance with Laws and Regulations

Provide Adequate Security and General Controls Over Financial Management Systems

The Service has made substantial efforts with limited resources to comply with OMB Circular A-130 and acknowledges that it needs to make improvements. The Service believes that the actions outlined in our response to finding D. in the Report on Internal Controls will correct the issues that led to this finding.

The Service appreciates your considerations concerning our comments. If you have any questions or need more information, please contact the Assistant Director - Business Management and Operations directly by calling (202) 208-4888.

Exhibit I

UNITED STATES FISH AND WILDLIFE SERVICE

Summary of the Status of Prior Year Reportable Conditions

September 30, 2001

Reference	Condition	Status
2000 – A	Undelivered Orders should be reviewed in a timely and comprehensive manner.	This condition has been corrected.
2000 – B	Construction-in-Progress reconciliation procedures need improvement in order to detect and correct errors in a timely manner.	This condition has not been corrected and is repeated in FY 2001
2000 – C	Reporting processes for grantees needs improvement to ensure grantees provide documentation to support costs incurred for Federal Aid Grants.	This condition has been corrected.
2000 – D	Capital equipment reconciliation processes need to be more effective.	This condition has not been corrected and is repeated in FY 2001
2000 – E	Procedures for recording capital equipment need to be improved.	This condition has not been corrected and is repeated in FY 2001
2000 – F	General controls over automated systems need improvement.	This condition has not been corrected and is repeated in FY 2001
2000 – G	Stewardship investments funded through grants for nonfederal physical property should be reported.	This condition has been corrected.

U.S. Department of the Interior
U.S. Fish & Wildlife Service

http://www.fws.gov

April 2002

www.ingramcontent.com/pod-product-compliance
Lightning Source LLC
Chambersburg PA
CBHW081230280526
45787CB00006B/2591